Cambridge Ele

Elements in Beckett S
edited by
Dirk Van Hulle
University of Oxford
Mark Nixon
University of Reading

CARNIVALS OF RUIN

Beckett, Ireland, and the Festival Form

Trish McTighe
Queen's University Belfast

CAMBRIDGE
UNIVERSITY PRESS

Shaftesbury Road, Cambridge CB2 8EA, United Kingdom

One Liberty Plaza, 20th Floor, New York, NY 10006, USA

477 Williamstown Road, Port Melbourne, VIC 3207, Australia

314–321, 3rd Floor, Plot 3, Splendor Forum, Jasola District Centre, New Delhi – 110025, India

103 Penang Road, #05–06/07, Visioncrest Commercial, Singapore 238467

Cambridge University Press is part of Cambridge University Press & Assessment, a department of the University of Cambridge.

We share the University's mission to contribute to society through the pursuit of education, learning and research at the highest international levels of excellence.

www.cambridge.org
Information on this title: www.cambridge.org/9781108965699

DOI: 10.1017/9781108963947

First published 2023

A catalogue record for this publication is available from the British Library.

ISBN 978-1-108-96569-9 Paperback
ISSN 2632-0746 (online)
ISSN 2632-0738 (print)

Carnivals of Ruin

Beckett, Ireland, and the Festival Form

Elements in Beckett Studies

DOI: 10.1017/9781108963947
First published online: January 2023

Trish McTighe
Queen's University Belfast
Author for correspondence: Trish McTighe, t.mctighe@qub.ac.uk

Abstract: Beckett's work is somewhat out of step with the logic of commemoration and celebration. Arts festivals, with their association with celebration, spectacle, and publicity, would not seem the ideal vehicle for Beckett's work. Yet that work has become highly festivalised, and the incongruities between it and festival forms provide a useful basis from which to examine both Beckett as festivalised commodity and festivals themselves. Festivalising Beckett in Ireland might be characterised as a way of bringing him back home, as well as a way of returning him to the canonical fold – he showed little interest in either during his later years, it need hardly be added. This Element examines Beckett's dissidence in the face of these imperatives of nation, home, and the canon, utilising Beckett's work in festival contexts to highlight, in the negative, the festival form.

Keywords: Happy Days Enniskillen International Beckett Festival, literary tourism, festivalisation, Enniskillen, Gate Theatre, Dublin, Irish culture

ISBNs: 9781108965699 (PB), 9781108963947 (OC)
ISSNs: 2632-0746 (online), 2632-0738 (print)

Contents

1 Introduction: Upon Ruinous Foundations

August 2015: I am on a forty-eight-seater bus travelling the narrow roads of the Fermanagh countryside to see Netia Jones's production of Beckett's late prose text *Stirrings Still*, created for the Happy Days Enniskillen International Beckett Festival (henceforth HDE). Enniskillen is a town located in the south-western corner of Northern Ireland, tucked just inside the hundred-year-old border that partitions Ireland. My journey on the bus is one of silent absorption in the landscape that I pass through, and an awareness of the bus smelling slightly of old school socks and stale sandwiches, a hint to its purpose when not ferrying Beckett-interested visitors around the hinterland of Enniskillen. Rocked by the motion of travel, I am dazzled by the richness of the green in the tree-lined fields, the sparkling blue of Fermanagh's many lakes glimpsed through breaks in the drumlins, all almost hyperbolically illuminated by a rare rainless day. I have just left the small town of Enniskillen which has been transformed almost every late summer since 2012 into a site of Beckettian homage, its sites dedicated to theatre, music, and visual art. Beckett's presence there is called into being through playful gestures from local businesses such as Beckett-inspired sandwiches and Beckett-style haircuts; the town transforms yearly into a canvas for Beckettiana. The bus takes us to a ruined barn on the Castle Archdale Estate where actor Ian McElhinney performs an accomplished still-ness, while Jones's elegant, monochromatic scenography converses with the dilapidated surroundings.

This performance event and the festival within which it occurred embody many of the features of Beckett festivals that I will explore in the following: the relationship between author, art and place, homage paid through visibility and spectacle, and the interweaving of the work with travel and tourism. It also encapsulates some of the juxtapositions between Beckett's work and the festival form: that of the distance to be travelled between celebration and ruination among the most important. In exploring the relationship between Beckett's aesthetic of sparseness and entropy and the celebratory spectacle of the modern arts festival form, it might be fitting to start here, among the ruins. The process of siting art in ruins, as happens with frequency at the HDE, a festival that forms one of the central case studies of this Element, fits within an aesthetic that itself commences from the nearly ruined, whether that be of architecture or of the body. Think of the 'Poor woman. All alone in that ruinous old house' who Maddy Rooney of *All that Fall* (1956) hears playing Schubert's *Death and the Maiden* (Beckett, 1984, 12). Or the ghostly May of *Footfalls* (1975), her body as flimsy as the worn carpet she paces in a house she has not left in years. Or even the peeling, fragmenting walls of the room in *Film* (1965) that Buster Keaton circles, desperately attempting to hold off perception of self by self. Bodies and places are promised to ruin in Beckett's work.

Such a grounding for an aesthetic seems at odds with festivals and with festivalisation, a word that describes an increased intertwining in the late twentieth century of art with economics, urban branding, and tourism (see Bennett et al., 2014, 1). When we celebrate an art such as Beckett's, what exactly are we celebrating? When the face of this notoriously shy author becomes a part of a city's brand, as I argue is the case with Dublin's 1991 and 2006 Beckett festivals, what exactly, aesthetically and ethically, is occurring? Both the content of the work, with its focus on failure, fading out, and fragmentation, and its form, privileging brevity and inconclusion, seem at odds also with the sorts of spectacles of cultural consumption that have become so important to Western culture in the late twentieth century. The same may be said of theatre. It often involves communitarian engagement, spectacle, consumption, and commodification. In Beckett's theatre work, many of the elements of theatricality are, in Anna McMullan's words, put 'on trial'. Beckett's theatrical practice, 'mounts a continual assault upon the structures of representation' and works 'against the assumption of any definitive position of authority from which to determine truth, meaning, or knowledge, for either characters or audience' (McMullan, 1993, 5). What questions, then, might such work pose for festivals?

This Element will focus in particular on the Beckett festivals connected to the Gate Theatre in Dublin, especially that of 1991 and of the 2006 centenary of the author's birth, and the HDE, which has been running almost annually since 2012. The broader questions that this Element will address are to do with the processes, institutional and ideological, of the festivalisation of Beckett's work, about the relationship between Beckett's work and the cultural economy, as well as about the nature of the festivals themselves.

Festivalisation is a major force shaping cultural consumption in the late twentieth and early twenty-first centuries. Emmanuel Négrier usefully describes it as:

> the process by which cultural activity, previously presented in a regular, on-going pattern or season, is reconfigured to form a 'new' event …. Festivalisation also describes the process by which cultural institutions, such as a cinema, theatre, arts centre or gallery orients part of their programme around one or more themes or events, concentrated in space and time. Festivalisation therefore results in part from the explosion of festivals, but also from some 'eventalisation' of regular, cultural offers. (2015, 19)

Festivalisation also describes 'an economically attractive way of packaging and selling cultural performance and generating tourism' (Bennett et al., 2014, 1), and as a means of branding urban centres as tourist destinations, and emphasising the 'the corporate attractiveness of "creative cities"' (Knowles, 2020b, 1).

The term has pejorative implications therefore and has been deployed to describe an over-commodification of cultural goods through festival-related tourism and place-marketing narratives (Getz, 2010, 5). Festivalisation functions as both descriptor of the ways in which culture is packaged in the latter part of the twentieth century and as a critical term to engage with the discursive and ideological aspects of festivals. This may be used to pinpoint the use of festivals for branding at the cost of deeper, long-lasting solutions to urban problems or meaningful connections with the specificities of their host locations (see Quinn, 2010, 271). It may also help to unpack underlying assumptions and ideologies of festivals and to query their relationship to existing class and other inequalities (Waterman, 1998, 64). Throughout this study, I utilise the term to describe how Beckett's work (and identity as an author) is 'eventified' (Hauptfleisch et al., 2007, 39) within varying festivals and therefore opened up to various interweaving ideological imperatives of nationalism and commodification, as well as those of city-branding, tourism, and place-marketing.

The way that Dublin staged Beckett and Beckettiana during the 2006 centenary demonstrates an important relationship between space, place, and aesthetics within festivals while also flagging up how festivals play a role in city branding and place-marketing. The combination of journey, site, and aesthetic event at the HDE indexes questions of time, aesthetic absorption, and the touristic economy. These festival events demand critical engagement with questions of cultural value and the way in which authorial presence is invoked and utilised within a broader tradition of biographical or single author-focused festivalisation. They also exemplify how authorial presence is called into being through various gestures; in Dublin, this included photographs of Beckett's face festooning city spaces, while in Enniskillen, the playful gestures of Beckett-inspired sandwiches and haircuts are accompanied by a Beckett-flavoured animation of its urban and rural landscapes.[1] These examples offer insights into the way that Beckett is 'read' and understood through festival production and also offer grounds for a consideration and indeed theorisation of the festival within modern and neoliberal Western cultures.

Irish festivals in particular allow for an examination of certain questions about the nature of the ideological forces shaping festivals, but it is important to stress at the outset that this is not the only possible approach or perspective on the matter. In the coming pages I trace a broader history of interactions between

---

[1] The most recent of these includes a staged reading of *Godot* sited at a remote, mountain border region near Enniskillen, where Anthony Gormley's *Tree for Waiting for Godot* (2013) marked the border line between the north and south of Ireland. The production was held at this site in 2018; see Maprayil (2018) for a detailed review.

Beckett's work and festivals, and these point to potential further studies looking at the festivalisation of Beckett within French, UK, and international contexts. It is important to note that the Gate Beckett Festival of 1991 had touring links with both London and New York, the 2006 Centenary saw separate celebrations in London, New York, Tokyo and Paris, as well as Dublin, while the HDE also has Paris links. The present study does not have the scope to address all these international Beckettian contexts, but it is hoped that this Element will signal to questions that might be asked and the approaches that might be taken to the notion of a 'global' festivalised Beckett.

For the purposes of this present study, the Irish goings-on (north and south) present both compelling and ample case study material, with a rich seam of events from which to mine a broader understanding of the relationship between the figure of the author and the festival milieu. The Gate festival work is representative of a specific phase in the late twentieth-century commodification of culture and city-branding. As a case study, it shows how culture begins to play a highly visible role in the process of 'enhancing cultural capital through cultural performance' as Richards and Palmer put it. They argue, somewhat optimistically – and perhaps uncritically – that 'cities which successfully harness cultural events as an integral part of a broader development strategy will reap the benefits of generating wider cultural, social and economic benefits. Eventfulness should not be an aim in itself, but a means of improving the city and making it more attractive and liveable' (Richards and Palmer, 2010, 4).

Ireland reflects readily this late twentieth-century turn to the construction of culture as capital of varying sorts and presents a genealogy since the 1950s of festivals being used for place-marketing. The reliance of the Irish economy on tourism for much of the twentieth century means that it is an ideal case study site to investigate the intertwining of culture, nation, place-making and marketing, and the arts. Furthermore, the HDE presents an opportunity to consider a festival that occupies a relatively marginal geographic location and one that is situated across the border that partitions the island of Ireland. Beckett's biography, connected to both Dublin and Enniskillen, means that a study of the tensions between the work and the festival form, the processes of cultural homage, and the mobilisation of national identity within festivals might begin here. Although Ireland might not be the only site of Beckett's festivalisation, it is an ideal staging ground to commence its study for these reasons. The following will seek to do justice to the richness of the work and complexities that these events manifest while acknowledging that this is but one strand of the study of the globalisation of Beckett.

Beckett did not write specifically for festivals, yet his work has found itself homed, with varying degrees of comfort, within festivals, both during his lifetime and posthumously. This is both to do with the increasing ubiquity of the festival form in later twentieth-century arts production and to do with the increasing brevity of Beckett's work from the 1960s on. While there may be dissonances between the work and the ethics and aesthetics of festivals, Beckett's oeuvre at the same time lends itself very effectively to this form. Furthermore, in true Beckettian spirit, such dissonance may be the very engine of productive estrangement, in that the figure of the festivalised Beckett may function as a deconstructive gesture unravelling the festival as we know it, getting under its ideological skin and pinning its more nebulous elements to the dissection table.

The field of festival studies is as vast and disparate as festivals themselves. In the immediate decades following World War II, the festival form emerged as one of the most viable ways to package cultural products within the late twentieth and early twenty-first centuries. A wide variety of cultural products can be found in festival form, in a diversity of festival locations, and with a breadth of differing communities attracted to these. In the delivery of artistic goods, the festival frame tends to fall into the background. All of this suggests that any attempt to present a unifying theory of festival and festivalisation would seem both foolhardy and nigh impossible. Narrowing the focus specifically onto arts festivals, this Element will engage with, therefore, what Nicholas Johnson has articulated as the dissonances between what a festival says and what it does (2017). This includes the discordance between the ideological veneer of the marketing strategy and glossy programme, for instance, and the material reality which underpins these, as well as those dissonances between the festival form and the content of the work festivalised (not to mention the character of the author). Approached in this way, we may see the festival form in the negative, witnessed through its opposites – quietude instead of spectacle, isolation instead of communitarian celebration, and ruin instead of product.

In splicing festivals and ruins, I am responding to the fact that many HDE events take place on the sites of literal ruins. I am also invoking *The Capital of the Ruins*, Beckett's report commissioned by RTÉ in 1945 on the town of St- Lô in Normandy, where he had volunteered with the Red Cross at the end of World War II. While doubt remains over whether or not the report was ever broadcast (for a recent analysis of this, see Davies, 2017, 171), it is the case that as a document, it singles out a similar sort of rhetorical concision, and situates us in a particular moment of post-war reconstruction. Many of the festivals that function as reference points for this Element came into being in that era of post-war reconstruction: the Edinburgh Festival, Avignon, and, closer to the current geographic area of focus, the Dublin Theatre Festival. This era signalled the emergence of the culture of festivals that has shaped cultural production in Europe in the latter part of the twentieth century. Julie Bénard notes the contradictory elements that shaped Beckett's 'Capital' piece:

> Despite what its title may intimate, *The Capital of the Ruins* does not depict a town in ruins but the way a community engages in re-construction after war. Though the report largely remains factual, it also foregrounds its own potential failure. What is at stake is not so much what is shown – representation –, but the potential failure of representation. (2018, online)

The concision of capital, the head or most important element of a thing, with ruins, the end-stage decay of a thing, provides the means by which we might think through the oddness of the relation contained in the phrase 'a Beckett festival', and all the representational failures that may imply. The HDE may literalise ruin in its programming, but in a sense all Beckett festivals commence from this point, the 'ruins' that comprise his oeuvre. As I discuss in the following, the festival form features heavily in the arc of Western history; an anthropological perspective would suggest that there is some shared and indeed cross-cultural human impulse towards community and ritual (see Falassi, 1987). But the festival as we know it, in its late twentieth-century form comprised of the commodification and packaging of culture, reflects an era mobilising culture for post-war renewal and reconstruction. This is not to suggest that there were no festivals prior to World War II. Indeed, the genealogies of modern festivals may be seen from multiple perspectives. One might look to Wagner's Bayreuth Festival, or to the history of carnival practices, or one might also look to the emergence of commemorative activities around specific writers – Shakespeare for instance – or one might observe both the emergence of leisure practices and its connection to the modern impulse to show, see and tell in, for example, the Great Exhibitions of the nineteenth century. A further strand might resist the Eurocentric origin story of festivals altogether and look to indigenous cultures as a means to understand festivals in their global context (see, for instance, Knowles, 2020a). While a number of these strands are reflected within this present study, the focus is primarily on the post–World War II moment that led to the creation of certain types of arts-focused festivals with characteristics that leave a determinable legacy upon cultural production in the global north today.

Just as institutions such as the European Union (as the EEC) and the United Nations came into being out of the ruins of post-war Europe, so too does the festival form as we know it.[2] Jen Harvie writes that the Edinburgh International

---

[2] Alongside Edinburgh and Avignon, the Festival of Britain may be noted here also; although this is somewhat more in step with the sorts of nationalist projects that happen in Ireland in the 1950s,

Festival (EIF) arose after World War II, at least in part, 'to bolster a badly damaged sense of European identity by supporting the post-war revival of European arts and culture' (2003, 14) and to serve as 'a kind of post-war rallying point' (Lord Harewood, quoted in Harvie, 2003, 14). She notes in the festival the commitment to 'promoting "the best" that was pervasive in Britain's post-war cultural climate' (Harvie, 2003, 15), while also connecting with Europe. This commitment to 'the best' saw the inaugural festival include Shakespeare productions accompanied by Molière and Giraudoux (16). Jean Vilar's Festival d'Avignon emerged out of 'the strong post-war impetus to break the conservative Parisian monopoly on artistic and theatre practices' (Wehle, 1984, 52). But while Edinburgh arguably utilised the founding works of European culture as a means of re-establishing the concept of shared European cultural heritage (the pedigree of which was, unquestionably, established by an elite culture), Vilar instead believed that 'a genuinely democratic public was essential to Avignon's success', a populist impulse amplified by his appointment as Director of the Théâtre National Populaire in 1951 (Wehle, 1984, 55). Broadly speaking, each of these festivals signals a particular understanding of the role of culture relative to post-war reconstruction, with Vilar's work most focused on the democratic potentials of collective cultural engagement. Over the decades, tourism and travel have become important aspects of these festivals. At Edinburgh, 12 per cent of tickets are sold overseas (Edinburgh Evening News, 2018, online), and in 2019 (pre-Covid-19 pandemic) ticket sales totalled three million (Snow, 2019, online), while 6.6 per cent of roughly 150,000 Avignon attendees hail from abroad and 75 per cent of all attendees come from outside Avignon (Turk, 2011, 261). These festivals, still running today, exemplify the beginnings of a European genealogy of festival cultures.

Considering their post-war context, it is clear that festivals can provide avenues for the continual remaking and reconstructing of culture and identity. They may be understood in this regard in light of Jacques Rancière's notion of the 'distribution of the sensible'. For Rancière, the dominant order in society shapes the distribution (*partage*) of the sensible forming 'the system of self-evident facts of sense perception that simultaneously discloses the existence of something in common and the delimitations that define the respective parts and positions within it' (2004, 12). *Partage* relates to what can be deemed worthy of representation as well as the ways in which space and time are shared and distributed among the people. One can see how festivals – in choosing to programme one artwork over another, or give time over to commemorate one

---

discussed in Section 3, it emerges against the same backdrop of crisis as the EIF, and it was seen as an opportunity to expand tourism and to publicise Britain's recovery and achievement to the world (see Festival of Britain, 1952, 15).

artist over another, in affording access (or not) to particular spaces – play a part in the ideological determination of the seen and heard. For Rancière, a rupture in the expectation of what is usually seen and heard can occur through aesthetics. My exploration will be alive to both what is rendered invisible in the processes of festivalisation as well as what is ruptured or exposed. Illumination of this requires careful attention to the differences that lie between varying festivals, the places they take place, the communities they serve, and the political and ideological worlds they are enmeshed within – those specificities of various festivals that make a unifying theory of the festival impossible. This may be also where the potentials of festival lie – in their radical openness and ostensibly democratic modes of participation.

In addressing these issues, this Element will look firstly at Beckett's own attitude to publicity and public spectacle, before moving to a consideration of a specifically Irish genealogy of festivals and festivalisation. The body of the analysis will draw on the case study examples of the Gate Theatre festivals and the HDE, examining each of these relative to their spatial and temporal practices. Throughout, I maintain focus on the structure of the festival in question, its ideological underpinnings and cultural contexts, and the manner in which it 'eventifies' the body of work in question. While not the sole focus, this study is alive to the sorts of questions that emerge from festival studies on notions of assembly and community. The 'collective commitment to an event' that festivals foster (Zaiontz, 2018, 2) is addressed in the Element's conclusion.

2 More Ruins: The Festival and the Author's Face

Celebration and commemoration: these are practices that we associate with festivals of all sorts but especially with biographical festivals. Within such festivals, the life of an author and their body of work is made visible while their status relative to the canon, and frequently their connection to a particular place, is confirmed. To be deemed festivalisable is to have a certain status conferred upon one's work. However, from a biographical perspective, the processes by which festivalisation makes visible, draws attention to, and displays seem greatly at odds with an author such as Beckett, whose negative attitude to public appearance and authorial spectacle is well documented. Examining the history of his work illuminates just how frequently it was included in various festivals, in spite of the author's shyness. Therefore, thinking through Beckett's attitude to publicity alongside the regularity with which his work has been festivalised unveils an apparent tension, one which calls for further exploration.

The receipt of the Nobel Prize for Literature in 1969 might be seen as the nadir of Beckett's relationship with publicity, with both he and his wife Suzanne famously regarding it as a 'catastrophe' (Knowlson, 1996, 570). In a letter to Barbara Bray from the Tunisian hotel he was staying in when the news broke, he declared that he is 'overcome by mail' and 'by the effort now and then to look pleased' (Beckett, 2016, 188). The correspondences that followed the Nobel drowned out any attempts at working, as he wrote a few days later to Bray: 'Until all this is out of the way, if it ever is, I can't work, which I know is of little importance, but to me the most important' (195). Hannah Simpson argues brilliantly that Beckett's later play *Catastrophe* (1982) echoes the sensation of exposure and vulnerability that comes with the prize: *Catastrophe*, she suggests, 'performs bodily exposure in a manner that mimics Beckett's own experience following the announcement of his Nobel laureateship'. She notes that Jérôme Lindon, Beckett's French language publisher, told the Nobel press: 'Chaque fois qu'un importun parvient jusqu'à l'écrivain, celui-ci est malade pour une semaine' ['Every time someone manages to importune Beckett in person, he is ill for a week'] (quoted in Simpson, 2018, 343). The Nobel can be read as a most public signalling of Beckett's aversion to publicity.

While the festivals that I discuss later in this Element took place posthumously, there are a number of salient examples of festival packaging of Beckett's work done during his lifetime. For instance, in the early days of Beckett being performed in London, we see a 1957 gala performance of *Fin de partie* as part of a French Festival week in London. This comes at a moment of what Dan Rebellato describes as British theatre's 'love affair' with French playwrights (1999, 128–9). Matthew McFrederick points out that no other London theatre has programmed productions of Beckett's plays as consistently as the Royal Court (2016, 72), while S. E. Gontarski suggests that his collaboration with Court director George Devine was among his most significant, alongside his work with Roger Blin and Alan Schneider (2016, 22). The Court's support and the relationships forged there, with director George Devine and designer Jocelyn Herbert, were pivotal for his career as a playwright (McFrederick, 2016, 72). London, McFrederick suggests, 'arguably proved to be the city where his reputation was sustained and supported, particularly at key phases of its development or against external pressures, a matter most evident through the staging of Beckett's double bill in 1957' (55). In 1957, as Beckett was struggling to find a theatre to host the premiere of *Fin de partie* and *Acte san paroles*, Devine and the English Stage Company at the Royal Court stepped in to host the French language premiere; this proved to be, in Gontarski's words, a watershed moment for Beckett (2016, 23). McFrederick writes that, 'This two week celebration epitomised how Devine was keen to support a European strand within his programming and demonstrated his own Francophile interests, which stemmed from his childhood excursions to France, his fluency in French and his previous theatrical work with Michel Saint-Denis' (2016, 56).

Less discussed in this context is how this presents an early example of the festivalisation of Beckett's work. The creation of a 'French Fortnight' becomes a means through which non-Anglophone and translated European work might be made legible and packaged for the London stage, as well as informing cultural relations: the *Fin de partie* run included a gala performance with the French ambassador in attendance (Gontarski, 2016, 22–3). As well as indexing Beckett's internationalism at the time, this also provides an example of the festival as a means of cultural packaging and intercultural translation, demonstrating how events such as these become ways of mediating culture across national boundaries. The work is also indicative of a broader trend of interest and appetite among London's playgoers for European work, which the Francophile Devine was well placed to feed. Beckett became a central part of these plans, which saw plays by Brecht, Ionesco, Sartre, Genet, and Arrabal all performed at the Court (McFrederick, 2016, 57).

By the 1970s, Beckett was well established as an author for the stage, and the years leading into the 1980s were peppered with public celebrations of his work of one sort or another. A survey of the letters of that time reveals several salient events that came to the author's attention. James Knowlson curated a Beckett exhibition in May-July 1971 at Reading and the University of East Anglia, at news of which Beckett was both 'honoured and embarrassed' (Beckett, 2016, 238). In November 1972, the New York Lincoln Centre Beckett Festival opened with a production of *Krapp's Last Tape* accompanied by the premiere of *Not I* performed by Jessica Tandy, though the latter was, to Beckett at least, 'imperfectly tested' (302, n. 2). Earlier that same year Beckett refused Knowlson's proposal for a biography with characteristic reticence and humility: 'There are lives worth writing, mine without interest in itself or relevance to the work is not one of them' (277). He refused with even more vehemence to have anything to do with Deirdre Bair's biography (298–9). The 1970s sees the continuation of Beckett's relationship with the Royal Court in London with a Beckett season presented there in 1976 in honour of the author's seventieth birthday (Gontarski, 2016, 36). In a further confirmation of reputation, *Godot* was taken into repertory at the Comédie-Française (Beckett, 2016, 449).

In 1979, Tom Bishop proposed a festival to celebrate Beckett's seventy-fifth birthday. Replying to Bishop, Beckett again provided a familiar response to such a proposal:

Let me say that I do not oppose yr. project of the Festival in Paris next Spring, because I feel you are keen to [do] it. And at once add that a respite from me & my work appears to me desirable. In my absence in any case. And for yr. own sake too think again. It would [be] an exhausting job & you should take advantage of yr. sabbatical to unwind and rest.

(Beckett, 2016, 507)

He later communicated his thanks to Bishop, even though intending to be absent from Paris during the celebrations (558, n. 1). In relation to the international symposium organised by S. E. Gontarski in Columbus, Ohio, for the same birthday he wrote to Jocelyn Herbert of his dread of 'the year now upon us and all the fuss in store for me here, as if it were my centenary. I'll make myself scarce while it lasts, where I don't know. Perhaps the Great Wall of China, crouch behind it till the coast is clear' (541). After returning from a challenging time with *Quadrat* in Stuttgart he expressed his exhaustion to Alan Schneider: 'Returned to Paris to an avalanche of mail from which 1 am only beginning to emerge, far from unscathed. My only desire for weeks to come is to sit quiet contemplating my old friend, empty space. It can't be published, the desire I mean' (550). The sentiment is further lyrically and poignantly expressed to David Warrilow in 1985: 'I continue to huddle in my corner trying in vain to agree with Descartes that bene qui latuit bene vixit. A bit late in the day' (664). The phrase translates as 'he who his hidden himself has lived well' and is adapted from a line in one Descartes's letters, reportedly what the philosopher wished for his gravestone (664, n. 2).

While the public honours and commemorations increased, Beckett's attitude to publicity remained unchanged. The position seems on the face of it incongruous with the spectacular nature of festivals and public commemorative events. One of the few texts that seeks to address this apparent incongruity is Stephen Dilks's *Samuel Beckett in the Literary Marketplace*, in which the author attempts, as Gontarski has it in his foreword, to unpack 'what he takes to be Samuel Beckett's complicity, not only in the business of the marketing of his books, but in the shaping and marketing of his own image as an ascetic, anticommercial artist' (2011, xiv). Dilks presents Beckett's dislike for publicity as 'one of the most powerful myths in Beckett studies' (1) and, invoking Raymond Williams, he sees in Beckett an 'anti-bourgeois stance of modernism' that achieves comfortable 'integration into the new international capitalism' (6). Dilks's argument, however, is both overstated and underpinned by a wilful misunderstanding of the nature of shyness. Shyness is often perceived to involve the avoidance of company and of spectacle, as sociologist Susie Scott writes, but in fact it 'embodies dramaturgical concerns about losing face, disrupting the interaction order and being rejected' socially (Scott, 2007, 12). It does not necessarily amount to cynical or knowing manipulations, rather, as Scott puts it, shyness often comes with 'a remarkable commitment to social solidarity and collective identity' (12). This is something which many of his friends attested was a characteristic of Beckett's personality. On the one hand then, we can read the festivalisation of Beckett's work as frequently inconsistent with the author's desire to remain out of the spotlight. On the other hand, however, Becket's tolerance for celebrations of his work was entirely consistent with his unwillingness to be publicly present and this has been the case for many shy authors. The history of Beckett's interaction with public celebration is a litany of commemorations *in absentia*. Shyness itself may be the grounds or stimulus out of which a great deal of art emerges, as Joe Moran suggests (2016, 163). The desire to have control over one's image is also highly consistent with diffident personalities.

More salient to a discussion of festivals is the loss of control over one's image that they threaten, as well as the absorption of the work into various cultural economies and towards unintended uses.[3] Festivals frequently operate at the limits of Beckett's (or his Estate's) control over narrative and image. As noted in the introduction to this Element, April 2006 in Dublin saw Beckett's face adorning the city. The centenary celebrations ran for two months during which time Beckett's by-then iconic visage, as photographed by John Minihan, seemed to hang on every street corner. Control over the uses of personal imagery, even by one's Estate after one's death, necessarily gives way in the wake of fame, and in the face of the marketing machinery of festivalised commemoration of the late twentieth and early twenty-first centuries. This is not to suggest that the content of the 2006 centenary or the work of the Gate on Beckett was anything but respectful homage. The Gate Theatre's then-artistic director Michael Colgan received Beckett's approval in the late 1980s to produce his work and to create a Beckett festival. Beckett's attitude to Ireland had begun to soften by that time. Of the Gate, Beckett wrote to Mary Manning Howe in 1986 that he saw 'the odd young Dubliner here, RTE & lately Gate. An improvement on our old lot if I remember right' (Beckett, 2016, 672), and later commented to Manning Howe:

---

[3] This might apply also to the ways that Beckett's work has been appropriated within corporate cultures. Notable examples of such misplaced appropriations include 'Think Different', Apple Company's ad campaign from the late 1990s which features Beckett's image, or the adoption of the 'fail better' line within the business-speak of the tech start-up world, see Marshall (2017, online). The increased referencing of Beckett within online spaces during the 2020/21 Covid-19 pandemic and lockdown presents a more recent example of popular appropriations of the work with, as Johnson notes, #waiting, #failbetter, #on circulating the Internet at increased rates during that time (2021, 256).

'Pleasant contact with some young or youngish Irish'. He named these as Seán O'Mórdha, who had made a documentary on Beckett's life (*Samuel Beckett: Silence to Silence*, 1991), author and critic Gerry Dukes, as well as Eoin O'Brien, author of *The Beckett Country*, and actor Barry McGovern, whose prose adaptation (with Gerry Dukes), *I'll Go On*, Beckett approved (Beckett, 2016, 692).

The Gate's festival of 1991, coming just two years after the author's death, reformed the public connection between Beckett and Ireland, and Irishness to a degree. These were author- or Estate-sanctioned events that sought to bring a sense of Irishness to the work while also balancing its European and international qualities. John Harrington notes that with its international collaborations the Gate's 1991 festival did not accept the notion of the 'Irish Beckett' wholly uncritically (Harrington, 2008, 136), and David Clare sees Colgan's diverse and international cast and creative team as reflective of the tensions between the 'local and the global' that mark Beckett's oeuvre (Clare, 2016, 50). Even in maintaining these tensions, however, the spectacle linking author to place in such a marked manner through the use of his face seems at odds with the personality of that same author. I will return to the questions raised about nationality and the national canon by the work of the Gate in the next section, but for now it is worth considering two examples of Beckett's direct interaction with festivals, one of which provides insight into the author's relationship with Ireland in the 1950s.

Beckett's notable and negative interactions with festivals include an issue with the Dublin Theatre Festival in the late 1950s and the bad feeling around the premiere of *Catastrophe* at the Festival d'Avignon in 1982. The Dublin Theatre Festival situation arose because the then Archbishop of Dublin, John Charles McQuaid, had raised objections to the inclusion of work by Joyce and O'Casey in the 1958 festival programme (see Pilkington, 2001, 157–8). In a letter in early 1958 to director Alan Simpson, Beckett queried if there is some truth to the rumours of the removal of Joyce's and O'Casey's work (Beckett, 2014, 102–3), and a month later wrote again to Simpson confirming the withdrawal of his work from the festival (106). In a letter to Carolyn Swift, Simpson's wife, he declared that 'as long as such conditions prevail in Ireland I do not wish my work to be performed there, either in festivals or outside of them' (112). As Harrington notes, when Beckett wrote to Simpson, he made reference to the 'Dublin Theatre "Festival"', with sarcastic quotes to emphasise his derision for an 'insufficiently modernised' Dublin that was still subject to the 'conditions of censorship that prevailed in the first half of the century' (2008, 132–3). It is Dublin and the very notion of it producing a festival that is under fire here. He rescinds the ban in 1960 with an apology to Simpson 'for the inconvenience I have caused you', saying it was 'time I fell off my high Eire moke' (Beckett, 2014, 332–3). Even though Beckett's antipathy towards Ireland is well documented and peppers his early work,[4] it is in 1959 that he accepts an honorary doctorate from Trinity College Dublin. In a notable (although pre-Nobel fame) example of public honours, he even attended the ceremony. As Knowlson describes it, 'almost everyone he had ever known in Dublin seemed to be there to shake his hand' and he enjoyed himself in spite of all (1996, 470).

Somewhat contrastingly, Beckett's experience with the Festival d'Avignon was to do with the dramaturgical choices made with *Catastrophe*. On seeing clips of the production televised, he expressed dismay to his director-collaborator Alan Schneider: 'brief flash of the Protagonist all trussed up with screaming white bonds to facilitate comprehension' (Beckett, 2016, 584). Writing to Barbara Bray, Beckett noted the apologies that had come in on behalf of AIDA (Association Internationale de Défense des Artistes), at whose invitation Beckett had written the piece (589), and later from the director Stephan Meldegg, which Beckett describes as '3 pages of self-satisfied self-justification' (591). Even though the play *Catastrophe* demonstrates a seldom-seen level of explicitness in Beckett's writing, his reaction to the Avignon festival production was quite similar to his reactions to other wayward productions.

Therefore, while neither of these examples is indicative of Beckett's feelings about festivals in general, they are indicative of the author's complex relationship with Ireland on the one hand, and commitment to authorial control and textual precision on the other.

In that regard, the Gate Theatre's festival, for instance, for all that it arrived in the world with Beckett's blessing and committed itself to the maintenance of authorial intention, mediated Beckett's Irishness in specific ways. The Dublin Centenary celebrations capitalised on the author's image in a manner hardly in keeping with the shyness of his persona. Institutional responses such as the Irish government's minting of €20 *Godot*-inspired gold coin are indicative of festivalised and commemorative gestures that appear out of step with Beckett's work as one of penury and dispossession (Kennedy, 2009, 70). The HDE continues to forge a connection with a place that, despite the fact that Beckett attended Portora Royal School, is somewhat tenuous in its biographical linkages. In sum, festivals often engender differences: they are events that actively construct and reconstruct different versions of an author, bringing their work into consonance or tension with varying cultural

---

[4] The tipping point of that relationship with Ireland might have reached its apotheosis in the 1937 Sinclair–Gogarty trial in which Beckett was publicly described as a blasphemer (Knowlson, 1996, 278–9) and after which he was to settle permanently in France.

discourses and ideologies. As with live theatrical events, festivals are never neutral staging grounds for engagement with art, but rather actively curate and construct scenes and platforms through which, variously, art can be experienced in novel ways, literary legacies confirmed, and ties to places and communities negotiated and re-negotiated. Like the theatre industry, with which Beckett festivals are frequently associated, festivals tend to provide space for unruly interpretations of the work and novel reconfigurations of authorial image. This is highly apparent in the Irish context, as the next section explores.

3 Beckett as Irish Icon: A Genealogy of Festivalisation

Brian Singleton has drawn a link between the formation (and reformation) of the canon of Irish drama and the processes of festivalisation, with festivals providing diagnostic tools to identify whose work is valued at particular moments in time:

> Perhaps the simplest way of determining the canonical in Irish theatre is to isolate writers whose work has been 'festivalized', embraced by the trend of single-author marketing which recognizes that great theatre writers are the mainstay of Irish cultural capital. These writers and their works are celebrated by international recognition, and so by festivalizing their opus their lesser-known and less popular works can be consumed on the international markets, thus reinforcing their canonical status. (Singleton, 2004, 259)

Commemorations, including festivals, acknowledge cultural value in a public setting and in so doing confirm and maintain that value, and frequently perform gestures of identification, connecting an author or artist to a particular place, nation, or region. Such gestures are readily evident in the context of Irish approaches to Beckett but are visible in the festivalisation of other authors as well, notably Shakespeare (see Habicht, 2001; Kahn, 2001) and, since the early twentieth century, Shaw (see Everding, 1998). The Irish context presents a very pointed case study of interlinkages between festivals, especially biographical ones, nationalist projects, and tourism. This is because, as is visible in the 1950s in the Republic of Ireland, a lack of any significant native heavy industry coupled with an economic climate perpetuating poverty and high rates of emigration meant that the concision between these worlds is more visible than is the case in other contexts.

The relationship in Ireland between tourism, festivals, and national identity emerges during the post-war reconstruction period of the 1950s. Just as some of the major European festivals came into being at Edinburgh and Avignon during this time, Ireland too saw the emergence of important cultural institutions, notably the Dublin Theatre Festival, inaugurated in 1957, as well as an overall awareness of the potency of the arts for economic and cultural capital on the world's stage. It is here that the scene is set for the later festivalisation of Beckett's work.

Diarmuid Ferriter, among others, sees 1950s Ireland as a complex period wherein many of the tensions hitherto unspoken within Irish culture became pointedly visible. It was a time that saw a growing liberalism and a change in attitudes to matters such as Catholic-directed censorship, even if the church still held a great deal of power (2004, 464). For economist Liam Kennedy, even though 'the 1950s are etched in the popular imagination as a decade of crisis and stagnation', it was during this time that 'the foundations were laid for a decisive break with a mediocre past', with investment forming the basis for future development (quoted in Ferriter, 2004, 464). An Tóstal, for instance, was comprised of tourist-focused historical pageantry and was part of the beginnings of a project of internationalisation, both economic and cultural, that would shape Ireland in the decades to come. The word Tóstal translated meant 'pageant' or 'muster' but was rendered in English as 'Ireland at Home' (Furlong, 2009, 168–9) and was dedicated to fostering tourism. While, as noted in Section 2, the late 1950s sees yet another wedge driven between Beckett and Ireland by the problems with the Dublin Theatre Festival, it is notable that this decade is also the culmination of a time in which the seeds for further growth were planted. As Brian Fallon recognises, the Gate Theatre had given 'an impetus to writers, actors and producers in the 1930s, a time when the Abbey, Ireland's national theatre, appeared to have lost its original spirit of adventure' and creativity, and 1943 saw the founding of the Irish Exhibition of Living Art, which became 'an annual for Irish Modernism and encouraged a new of generation painters and sculptors' (1998, 13). Notably, Louis le Brocquy, who would later go on to design the set for the Gate's iconic production of *Godot*, came to prominence in the mid-1950s.

By the 1950s, tourism, and its links with cultural pageantry, festivalisation and public culture in general becomes one of the means by which a previously insular and protectionist Ireland now began to open to foreign investment and join the beginnings of an emergent global tourist market. Tourism revenue began to rise from the late 1950s (Meenan, 1970, 85) and the economy moved away from protectionism, a sentiment reflected in the application for Marshall Aid after World War II (Ferriter, 2004, 467). Much of this was down to the efforts of Seán Lemass, then Minister for Industry and Commerce, who saw tourism as an 'export business of the highest value' (quoted in Pilkington, 2001, 154). Overall, it can be said that the 1950s 'saw a resounding rejection of [the] economic nationalism' of the preceding decades (Foster, 1988, 577).

Ireland's post-war application for Marshall Aid (the US-funded European Recovery Programme) implied, as Roy Foster puts it, a readiness to engage in economic cooperation within Europe (577), moving away from the social and economic insularity of the post-independence state. Irene Furlong suggests these loans also helped concentrate the mind of the Irish government on the 'dollar potential of tourism' (2009, 213) and the promotion, in the minds of the Irish people, of its value. An Tóstal pageantry of the early 1950s provides a dramatic illustration of Lemass's commitment to tourism: in 1951 Juan Trippe, president of Pan American Airlines suggested to Lemass that a 'Come back to Erin' festival aimed at Irish Americans could provide a solution to the dollar problem – a comprehensive programme of sporting and cultural events with the support of Irish media and churches (Furlong, 2009, 168). The Tóstal pageantry was to be held in 1953 (169). With politicians like Lemass stressing the centrality of tourism to the Irish economy, these pageants became a means of, as Fitzpatrick Dean puts it, attracting tourists and creating 'a version of the Irish past that could involve thousands of citizens in performative supporting roles' (Fitzpatrick Dean, 2014, 222). Furlong concludes that although the event did not attract the hordes of American visitors that it had intended, and some of its activities, like the Dublin 'Bowl of Light', were furiously mocked (Furlong, 2009, 171–2), it left a legacy of cultural festivals and helped to foster increased concern for heritage and preservation (176–7). Even if the quality of the pageants meant that they were, in the words of A. J. Levanthal in the late 1950s, 'a rather inchoate jumble of national aesthetic jollifications illuminated by fireworks' (quoted in Fitzpatrick Dean, 2014, 222), there were some important outcomes, the legacy of which can still be seen to this day. The Yeats Summer School for example came into being from An Tóstal funding in 1960 as did the Dublin Theatre Festival in 1957 (242).

Fitzpatrick Dean sees in the creation of the Dublin Theatre Festival the understanding among Tóstal planners of the potential of Irish theatre to attract international tourists (2014, 189). Ireland's most famous theatre could not at the time fulfil that role, given its temporary residence at The Queen's after the fire of 1952. Tóstal planners looked to pageantry initially, much of it ambitiously outdoors, given the Irish climate. As Fitzpatrick Dean has it, costs, logistics and risks led Tóstal organisers to consider other ways to include theatre; the Dublin Theatre Festival, inaugurated during the 1957 An Tóstal, was the result (222). It was much more successful than previous An Tóstal events, in spite of early controversies: its inaugural year closed with the suppression of the Pike Theatre's production of Tennessee Williams's *The Rose Tattoo* and the following year saw the 1958 Festival run-in with Archbishop McQuaid, after which Beckett temporarily withdrew permission to perform his plays in Ireland.

The dealings of the Irish state with the Pike over *The Rose Tattoo* was over a condom (illegal in Ireland) supposedly appearing on stage, though no such item was actually visible (see Swift, 1985; Whelan, 2002). The controversy and the legal battle that followed revealed, as Lionel Pilkington has it, 'a dramatization of the ideological battle that was taking place in the 1950s: between an expansionist state agenda (championed by politicians like Lemass and senior civil servants like [TK] Whitaker) and the defensive reactions of dominant elements within the Catholic church' (2001, 157).

The playwright Thomas Kilroy, reflecting on the 1950s, saw the debacle over the 1958 festival as absurd to such a degree that it was another step in the dismantling of censorship in Ireland, generating as it did great anger among the theatre community (Kilroy, 2013, 15). Morash sees in the Dublin Theatre Festival an internationalising effort, reflecting emergent economic policy in its 'rejoin[ing of] the wider theatre world' as it balanced home-grown work with touring world theatre (Morash, 2002, 222).

Beckett's pessimism about the Ireland that censored his work in the 1930s and that he saw as fundamentally narrow and retrograde was not unwarranted (see Kennedy, 2009, 56–7). Even if we regard the 1950s as signalling a nascent shift away from a narrow understanding of identity (Catholic, nationalist, agrarian) and from the fantasies wrought by politicians such as Éamon de Valera of Ireland as an innocent, pure, self-sustaining agrarian nation (for instance, see de Valera, 1943), the ways in which culture and economics become bedfellows in this era demands attention. The image of rural innocence, a people and place untouched by modernity, becomes the material of the iconography of the nascent tourism industry, as evidenced by Bord Fáilte campaigns and most emphatically visible in John Hinde's postcards (Furlong, 2009, 180).[5] Eric Zuelow comments on the shaping of Irishness itself within tourism discourses:

> For tourism developers these were positive attributes to be celebrated and encouraged. If the simple unsophisticated Irishman once served a colonial role by partly justifying English rule, he now functioned to illustrate unique characters of Irish people that not only fostered tourism but also helped to define the Irish as a singular culture and contrasted sharply with Ireland's more abrupt neighbours. (Zuelow, 2005, 195)

He points out that tourism is an ideal place to begin to examine the process of the construction of nationhood because 'at its heart, it is about selling and consuming national "difference"' (201). In Ireland, as in other places, it embodies the paradox of the presentation of the traditional and the modern – the image of

---

[5] See for example: www.johnhindearchive.com/index.php?Ireland#.YJUiuqHTXD4.

traditional Ireland becomes increasingly incongruous with modern Ireland (200). Tourism discourses also function to manage affect: Ireland was constructed as a place of welcomes, the sentiment literally referenced within the name of the tourist board ('fáilte' translates as welcome). This sense of a welcoming people reflects pride taken in Irish hospitality yet is also an affect shaped by material necessity: the need to welcome the tourist is both a product and a signifier of economic vulnerability.

Observing how many of the narratives of Irishness – the myths of the West, the Anglo-Irish legacy, and even the northern conflict – are 'appropriated by the tourism industry' (Duffy, 1997, 81) brings us neatly to that other aspect of the deliberate coupling of the arts and the economy that emerges in the 1950s in Ireland: the commodification and packaging of culture that sees the arts become an element of a nation's economic resource. Philosophers of modernity have observed and theorised this process in action in the earlier part of the twentieth century, with Theodor Adorno, together with Max Horkheimer in the 1940s, critiquing the emergence of what they term the 'culture industry'. While Horkheimer and Adorno in the 1947 *Dialectic of Enlightenment* were critiquing the ubiquity and uniformity of popular culture, their provocative tracing of the way that art 'takes its place among consumer goods' (2002, 127) offers a critical vocabulary through which the contemporary arts festival might be viewed. While the arts have always held a particular relation to the economy in various forms such as patronage, as Adorno and Horkheimer note, this era of aesthetic production sees any notion of the use value of art (including the usefulness of art's uselessness) being replaced by exchange value (128). Succumbing to ideology means concealing the contradictions that form between art and commodity. These writings form foundational critical wedges with which to probe the characteristics of festivals. Questions may be asked about the way that all festivals, including arts festivals, form a glossy veneer that, for example, may overlay unjust working conditions for festival workers and artists, urban problems and inequalities that permeate the spaces of the festival, or ignore ticket prices that mean the work of the festival is not accessible to all. What we see in festivals frequently is seen also in tourism: a smoothing over of the contradictions, antagonisms and unpalatable aspects of history, as well as the often-contradictory nature of the relations between art and the market.

The late twentieth-century festivalisation of Beckett sees a continuation of the pattern of the internationalisation and globalisation of Irish culture noted above. It reflects also how festivalisation and national belonging might be seen as interwoven while, as Section Four explores, demonstrating how art can become enmeshed with neoliberal ideological assumptions about culture, the economy, and place.

4 Festival Space: Staging the City

What might be noted through an examination of festivals themselves and the scholarly literature exploring them is that there is sometimes a struggle to materialise in meaningful ways the festival frame, whether that is exposing the festival as ideological veneer over the contradictions that shape it, or examining how a festival organises a viewer's perception of the artwork. There are a number of reasons for this. One of these is to do with festivals' 'poly-systemic' nature, their 'uneasy composite of (potentially) competing activities' (Hauptfleisch et al., 2007, 42), while the difficulty of documenting and analysing such poly-systems of live events presents another challenge. The object disappears in the moment of its creation, as Peggy Phelan notes of performance (1993, 146), and can only later be found in memory and the documents that make into to the archive – programmes, reviews, and other remains. The festival's evanescence, in tandem with the way it forms backdrops for art events to take place, means that it frequently remains in the background as a form, even if it provides the imagery and branding strategies to shape culture.

Even the process of festival reviewing itself is fraught. A festival reviewer produces a single perspective on a multitude of works; they may not see all the festival has on offer, depending on the size of the event and the volume of artworks – a review is a necessarily incomplete document, therefore. Brenda O'Connell and Nicolas Johnson offer a subtle, dialogic answer to the problem of festival reviewing in their 2014 review of the HDE. Taking Beckett's dialogues with Georges Duthuit as a structuring principle (Beckett, 1987), they articulate the challenges attached to what they are trying to do: the communication in the review of the 'Total festival, complete with missing parts, instead of partial festival', which tries to mirror also the fragmentary nature of this festival (and indeed the festival form) (O'Connell and Johnson, 2014, online). Through a staged conversation they offer a journey through the festivals of 2012 and 2013 while articulating the difficulty of containing a multifaceted event within text. Festivals might be said to be somewhat unruly entities, even if, as I discuss below, the operations of festivalisation frequently create conditions for the framing and ideological containment of art. What I will try to do in the following, however, is less to do with illuminating the nitty gritty of specific festival moments and details, but rather with how the festival 'frame' is also a spatial one, how festivals make room for certain activities and perspectives, even if frequently the festival frame itself disappears into the background. I initially take a bird's eye view survey of how the Gate festivals relate to the spaces of nation and to Dublin's urban centre, before looking at the ways in which the HDE moves its audiences through the spaces of the Fermanagh countryside.

The story of Beckett's work in festivalised form is, in an Irish context at least, one of a broader history of a shifting relationship with place, national identity, and cultural capital in that region over the course of the twentieth century. Examining Beckett's relationship with festivals in the Irish context is fruitful, precisely because of how homage becomes tinged with ownership, art becomes shaped by ideologies of nationhood, and public events are co-opted into national symbols and branding exercises. Festivals of Beckett's work in Ireland are marked in unique ways by contradictory and complex gestures of recuperation, as this section will explore.

While Beckett was produced fairly steadily in Ireland up until the early 1990s, often in theatre spaces like the Abbey Theatre's Peacock stage, a smaller space usually reserved for experimental or less 'popular' work, the Gate's 1991 festival presented the most large-scale and visible connection between Beckett and Dublin up to that point. This festival emerged from what was a longstanding theatrical institution founded in the early twentieth century and was primarily – though not exclusively – a theatre festival. The communitarian nature of theatre means that it frequently serves, as Steve Wilmer puts it, 'as a microcosm of the national community, passing judgement on images of itself' (2002, 2). This formation of community and nation via theatre is all the more visible in the Irish context, where theatre's role in the emergent national consciousness is literalised in the foundation of a national theatre movement in the late nineteenth century. For Abbey Theatre founders W. B. Yeats and Lady Gregory, such an institution was envisioned as a 'Celtic and Irish school of dramatic literature' for a people 'weary of misrepresentation' (quoted in Robinson, 1951, 2). Such finding or uncovering of identity is often a project for the imagination; in Christopher Murray's analysis the theatrical mirror gives back images, not of reality, but of a 'perceived reality' (2000, 9). Beckett's drama might present difficult terrain upon which to continue the Irish project of forming such a community. Both he (urban, Protestant, and middle-class) and his work (abstract, avant-garde) might be seen as what becomes excluded when the stability of the national narrative and the community (Catholic, nationalist, rural) which is formed in and through it is at stake. This festival grappled therefore with the 'tension between the local and abstract' (Clare, 2016, p. 50) and attempted to bring Beckett 'home' (Colgan, 1991) in the eyes of some, by uncovering the familiar and Irish within it, while at the same time looking to international resources and contexts, in terms of touring and professional collaboration. The Gate itself, as the second major Dublin theatre, does not carry the same responsibilities to the nation as does the Abbey, Ireland's national theatre (nor does it receive the same amount of public funding), and its history as a theatre for experimentation meant it was an ideal institution with which to navigate the complexities of national boundaries when it came to Beckett's work.

The posthumous festivalisation of Beckett came at a particular moment within Irish culture and its economic development. What was sown in the 1950s in economic policy began to bear fruit in the 1990s. The era saw not only a burgeoning sense of confidence in regard to economic prospects certainly but also a renewed vigour in terms of cultural activity and arts, as well as a potently articulated sense of identity. There are several contributing factors: the attraction of international investment is one, though it might be noted that this simply replaces a clerical, semi-theocratic system with a neoliberal one, the beginnings of the peace process in Northern Ireland/the north of Ireland and optimism on the island about an end to the by then two-decades-long conflict,[6] and more money entering government coffers to support the arts. By the 1990s, the Irish government was seeking to quantify the economic impact of the cultural industries in Ireland; this is reflected in a number of significant reports and papers (see, for instance, Coopers & Lybrand, 1994). If there was a growth in this time in artistic production there was also a growth in what Foster, perhaps uncharitably, has called a 'reclamation' of émigré Irish authors, Beckett among them. Foster notes that doubts about the nationality of one's writers is nothing new to Ireland, as the squabbles among obituarists over Yeats's literary and cultural identity following his death in 1939 shows (Foster, 2001, 94). The banned, like Joyce, and by implication here Beckett as well, have been reclaimed as Irish (110).

While due caution is needed not to overstate the case, suggesting that Beckett was somehow ignored or invisible in Irish culture up to this point, the process of the development of the Gate festival demonstrates a certain perception at the time that Ireland was somewhat irrelevant to Beckett and to events relating to the author. Take for instance the Irish reaction to the April 1986 festivities organised in Paris by Tom Bishop to celebrate Beckett's birthday. Although the events were covered in the Irish newspapers, there was a perception that the celebrations were poorly representative of Ireland and the Irish Beckett connection. *The Irish Times* Paris correspondent Lorna Siggins noted in early April how the accompanying symposium was to include no Irish speaker and there

---

[6] For the sake of brevity, throughout the rest of this Element I refer to this six-county region as Northern Ireland, but I acknowledge here its contested status. For many who identify as Irish and nationalist, the north of Ireland is a preferred title to indicate its continued connection to the Republic of Ireland. I address some of the complexities of space and identity in this region as they pertain to Beckett and festivals in Section 5.

was little by way of Irish offerings in the rest of the program, except for the O'Mórdha film *Samuel Beckett: Silence to Silence*. Although Barry McGovern and Gerry Dukes's prose adaptation *I'll Go On*, which Colgan produced, was performed in Paris at the same time, it was not part of the official festive programme. When it came to the 1991 Gate events, Colgan is cited by Jamie Dettmer as saying that Beckett's death in 1989 provided 'a new impetus' for the festival: obituaries for the author 'spoke of his death as a loss to France. Mr Colgan felt he should reclaim Beckett's Ireland' (1991).

John Harrington describes the 1991 Gate Beckett festival as having a 'cultural message' of 'reappropriation of the French existentialist as the Irish writer'. Harrington maintains however that the festival ultimately presented a complex interweaving of national and international theatre and literary scenes (2008, 136). Furthermore, as noted above, Beckett seemed well disposed to these Irish in comparison to the 'old lot' (Beckett, 2016, 672). It is clear, though, that an identity had begun to be forged by the aforementioned *I'll Go On*, the 1988 production of *Godot*, and the 1991 Beckett Festival which was to see the Gate become not only an international exponent of Beckett's work – frequently in festival form – but also part of the mechanism for reclamation of the exiles which was perceived to be a feature of Irish life at the time. As Foster puts it, commenting on the outgrowth of literary summer schools in Ireland in the latter years of the twentieth century, artists

> are reclaimed on behalf of those places, and on behalf of Ireland's newly asserted identification with them. As Ireland becomes a nation of immigrants rather than emigrants, it is repatriating its writers. They are being reinserted within what is conceived of as their appropriate borders: celebrated in the same way as people are often mourned, for the sake of the bereaved rather than the dead. (2001, 111)

If Foster's commentary seems somewhat overwrought, he is clearly keying into a certain anxiety over the ownership of literary icons and products, something that is also visible in scholarship from the 1980s and early 1990s that attempted to process Beckett's relationship with Ireland. McMullan notes that it was 'not until the 1980s that two journals, the *Irish University Review* (1984) and *Hermathena* (1986) published special editions on Beckett' and his Irishness began to become addressed in the criticism (2004, 90). For Rónán McDonald this signals a rather belated inclusion in the Irish canon (2009, 36). Eoin O'Brien's *The Beckett Country* was published in 1986 and marked the connection between Dublin landscapes and Beckett's texts, and John Harrington's *The Irish Beckett* and S. E. Wilmer's edited collection *Beckett in Dublin* were both published in the early 1990s. Such scholarship was frequently shaped by the careful attempt to map Beckett's biographical connection to Ireland and its fluorescence, in fragments, in his later work, while balancing the fragmentary and abstract aspects of the work. That attempt to 'map' Beckett's Ireland is one fraught with opposing desires, as David Lloyd articulates:

> Not to allow significance of a referential kind to the multifarious ways in which Irish matter appears in his work from start to finish, would be to yield to readings that see Beckett as saving literature for a pure and uncontaminated aesthetic and for a universal humanism .... On the other hand, the very attempt to grasp the ways in which Irish matter functions in Beckett ... tends to founder on the reef of ... insensitivity to or incompatibility with a work that is so resolutely antagonistic to representation or to any dialectical integration of part with whole. (2010, 37)

If scholarship sought to proceed gingerly in this direction, theatrical practices tend to be always already determined by local contexts and by the identifiable materiality of bodies. For perhaps that reason, cultural location formed one of the threads of discussion of the Gate festival's 1996 New York Lincoln Centre Festival tour. Michael Feingold's review noted the revelation of Beckett as irrevocably Irish that comes with these productions, finding that place and culture 'jumped out of these actors' mouths with a new agency (1996). Howard Kissel notes a similar effect but points out that the accents are 'unforced, natural accents, that is, not the brogue or lilt of the stage Irishman' and somehow form a 'logical counterpoint to the bleak undercurrents' of the work (1996, 49). The New York reviewers in 1996 were clearly considering questions of legacy, homage, and canonisation and how these were necessarily linked to the voices and bodies of the performers. Alexis Greene sees the Gate's work as precise and respectful of Beckett's stage directions, 'demonstrating how right the author was to insist on the kind of staging he wanted' (1996, 12). Martin Washburn commented that the Gate's efforts inclined towards canonisation with all the correctness of approach that this implies (1996, 77).

While the central characteristics of festivalisation are therefore observable within these festival events, the impulse towards homage is an important driver and should not be perhaps described reductively as marketing techniques or branding alone. The broader history of the Gate Theatre is worth noting here too: this is a theatre that in its early days from the 1920s provided a home for the sorts of experimental, avant-garde and international work that was not being played at that time at the Abbey. The Gate emerged in 1928 out of the Dublin Drama League, which was set up to introduce European modernist drama to Irish audiences in order, as Elaine Sisson puts it, 'to promote a vision of ... national life other than that of cottage and tenement' with the Abbey, as the national theatre, continuing to 'provide homespun rural dramas that reflected the ideologies of the traditional and the authentic'. The Drama League and later the Gate fostered an appetite for edgy, avant-garde representations of modern life (Sisson, 2011, 39). Pilkington cites a heavy focus in the 1940s and 1950s on the Irish language by the then artistic director at the Abbey, Ernest Blythe (2001, 139), with low production standards (143), and a tendency on Blythe's part to think of the theatre as being 'dedicated to the enactment of key *issues* relating to the Irish state' (165; emphasis in original). The Gate was a part of what might be seen as an alternative experimental tradition within Irish theatre.

When Colgan took over the running of the theatre in 1984, he was moving from a significant role in the running of the Dublin Theatre Festival that he described himself as 'elbowing' his way into (O'Toole, 2013). Gaining the role at the Gate involved a similar sort of elbowing and his ethos at that theatre meant a focus on what might be seen as 'classic' modern drama (mostly authored by men). It is worth noting that since the Gate does not receive the same arts funding as the Abbey, it has always had to work harder to stay afloat. Colgan took over the theatre at a time of severe financial instability and his acumen for programming what are known as 'bankers' was notable. Formative years at the Dublin Theatre Festival seemed to have left Colgan well-prepared for an understanding of the potency of festivalisation; authors such as Harold Pinter, David Mamet, and Brian Friel have all received festival billing.[7] The Gate also supported the work of Barry McGovern, whose stage adaptation of Beckett's novels in *I'll Go On* (1986) was a very successful rendering that has toured globally over the last thirty years. The 1991 festival grew out of Colgan's discussion with Beckett of a proposed production of *Waiting for Godot* that took place in 1988. With Beckett's injunction to 'keep it simple' ringing in his ears, that *Godot* production, with a set design by Irish artist Louis le Broquy, was highly successful and with a few cast evolutions became the anchor production for later festivals as well as a signature production of the play in the Irish and international contexts. For Colgan, the idea of a single core set to be used to stage nineteen of the plays (except for *Eleutheria*) within a short space of time became the pragmatic kernel of the idea for the festival. Interestingly, according to Colgan Beckett's only stipulation was that *Endgame* not be presented as a multiple bill (Woodworth, 1991).

There is not the space here to reprise some of the more intricate discussions of the productions at this festival. As noted, Harrington (2008) and Clare (2016) provide detailed and cogent analyses of the festival, particularly in relation to its

---

[7] A full list of the theatre's production since 1984 can be found here: www.gatetheatre.ie/past-productions/.

internationalism. I have previously addressed the construction of Beckett's relationship to Dublin's urban and rural landscape within the iconography of the Festival, especially regarding the use of the David Davison photographs from *The Beckett Country* (McTighe, 2018a). Gerry Colgan's reviews in *The Irish Times* form an important record of the details of the festival (see Colgan, 1991), as does Claudia Harris's account for *Theatre Journal* (1992). What I would like to highlight here is the visual legacy of this festival, in terms of the contribution of this festival to the image of Dublin, by which I mean both the visual iconography of the city as well as the city's reputational branding, with the latter most evident in the later centenary festival.[8]

As noted, connections between Beckett and Dublin were drawn in this festival aurally, through the vocality of the actors, and visually through the imagery from *The Beckett Country* that cites and indexes Beckett's Dublin, its photographs connected with fragments of text in the programme. Visual art played a role in this festival also; for example, an exhibition at the Douglas Hyde Gallery was devoted to works inspired by Beckett (Fallon, 1991). Much of this, along with the academic symposium that came as part of the festival, was not formally embedded in the programme. Such events and exhibitions become much more central to the programming by 2006 alongside a development of the connection between the visuality of these festivals and an emergent relationship between festivalisation and city branding.

The 1991 Gate festival was part of the Dublin Theatre Festival that year and these two connected festivals were part of Dublin's City of Culture festivities taking place across the year; this layering of festival events has a familiar ring to it by now, as festivals have become a significant means by which cities brand and market themselves. Furthermore, Harris opens her review of the 1991 Festival by commenting that 'Dublin realized its role as 1991 City of Culture in large measure because of the Gate Theatre's Beckett Festival' (1992, 405). The Dublin City of Culture project had had some problems fulfilling its aims. By August 1991, criticisms were being levelled at the organising committee of the festivities for being 'elitist, exclusively city-centre oriented, lacking in cohesion' and 'poorly publicised' (Battersby, 1991). There was a sense also, as is by now a familiar critique of festivals with international or global reach, of a lack of attention paid to local arts. With its relatively small budget, the Dublin festivities were accused of relying on work that was already planned or being

---

[8] Another visual legacy of this festival lies in the filmed versions of Beckett's theatre plays which Colgan spearheaded in 2001. While slightly uneven in quality, the 'Beckett on Film' project, sharing many of the original cast and directorial team as the 1991 festival, forms a kind of document of the festival work. Further details and critique can be found in Frost and McMullan (2003) and Dowd (2003).

done to complete the remit of the event; the Beckett festival received a mix of public and private monies with support from the Arts Council of Ireland, the Dublin City of Culture fund, the then state-owned airline Aer Lingus, and from the cultural institutes of Britain, France, and Germany (Woodworth, 1991). Its reach and scope made it a perfect signature event for the sort of internationalist ethos of City of Culture events.

Cities of Culture and other festivals are frequently interwoven with UNESCO heritage designations and become a means to drive tourist traffic to a place and 'stage' that place for the tourist gaze (d'Eramo, 2021, 97). Dublin received UNESCO City of Literature designation in 2010 and is part of the UNESCO Creative Cities network.[9] The strategic plan that accompanies this designation makes clear the intention to 'Devise a campaign of strong brand and identity development' and 'Enshrine the literary city in tourism plans' (Department of Arts, Heritage and the Gaeltacht, 2016, 5). As Nuala Johnson has noted, this 'imagining of Dublin as a literary space . . . provides a niche through which the city can be marketed while simultaneously inviting the traveller to journey through the city on the heels and through the lens of its literary characters. This literary tourism, cultivated officially through state agencies, is also promoted unofficially by literary atlases such as Bradbury's.' (2004, 95)

Literature and literary figures have formed the central spine of the city's international branding and are the ingredients for the 'promenade' theatre of the festival city. This is part of the way in which Beckett became registered within a Dublin spatiality. Literary tourism in general connotes a sort of haptic historiography connecting bodies in the present to those of the past. Take, for instance, the Dublin Literary Pub Crawl (www.dublinpubcrawl.com/), which connected place and authors while also offering visitors a window into these authors' infamous drinking habits. The Literary Pub Crawl tours have been in operation since 1988 and serve as an alternative, frequently night-life-focused, means of experiencing the city. Visitors are introduced to various details about the writers that frequented Dublin's city spaces (some but not all of them drinking establishments) through performance-lectures peppered with skits drawn from the work of the various authors: Joyce and Beckett are of course included, as are Oscar Wilde and Brendan Behan. The tour presents an exemplary concision of tourist movement and haptic literary history; it provides a telling example of the varying modes through which a city's tourism industry maps and constructs versions of that place. Such is the lifeblood of historical and literary tourism: touch the place, touch – somehow – the past, the person.

---

[9] See: www.dublincityofliterature.ie/about/dublin-unesco-city-of-literature/.

The places where this writer walked (or drank) regularly, or that writer created their masterpieces become, in Dean MacCannell's words, 'sacralized'. He writes of 'sight sacralization' (1999 [1976], 44–5) in which objects and sights are constructed as tourist attractions, and this can be adapted to express the 'site' sacralisation of literary tourism, in which the residue of the writer's presence feeds a the tourism imperative.

Literalised place connections formed a notable aspect of the 2006 Beckett Centenary Festival in Dublin. That event, it might be added, shared a great deal with the Bloomsday celebration of 2004, which marked one hundred years since the fictional date of Joyce's *Ulysses*. Bloomsday itself has run since 1954 and comprises a playful marking of the route taken by Leopold Bloom, the central character of *Ulysses*, as he makes his journey through the city. Adding to the palimpsest of literary heritages established in Dublin, the Beckett centenary saw a significant number of public artworks also marking the city. This includes publicly accessible exhibitions: Cian O'Loughlin's large-scale portraits inspired by Beckett's plays exhibited at the Office of Public Works, an exhibition at Dublin City Libraries together with the Department of Foreign Affairs traced the life of the author, there was a National Library exhibition of the John Minihan photographs of Beckett, and an exhibition entitled 'Samuel Beckett: Passion for Paintings' exhibition at the National Gallery. The festival's most pointed concision of author and place was a series of light projections on landmarks of Dublin city centre (and London's) by artist Jennie Holzer.

Holzer's work launched the month-long celebration, with a light show projecting selections of Beckett's texts across city centre spaces and buildings. Holzer is known for her work using light to project written statements, usually her own, on the walls of landmark public buildings (samples of her projects including her Dublin and London centenary work can be seen here: https:// projects.jennyholzer.com/projections). These large-scale visual art pieces tend to transform city sites into both pages or canvasses, with messages that are concise and provocative. In the lead up to the events, Holzer admitted to being daunted by the prospect of tackling Beckett's work, which she has long admired but feeling 'very strongly that this city is Beckett's home. In Dublin, his poetry of absurdity becomes rather literal' (Agence France-Presse, 2006). Holzer used fragments of relatively abstract text from Beckett's work (in London other authors were included also), including quotes from *The Lost Ones* (1970), *Enough* (1965), *Ill Seen Ill Said* (1981), *The Unnamable* (1953), *Company* (1979) and *Lessness* (1970). These fragments of texts were projected on city centre buildings with, for instance, extracts from *Ill Seen Ill Said* projected across the River Liffey so that the letters trailed off into the water. The text includes 'Grace to breathe that void. Know happiness', 'Seeing the black night or better blackness pure and simple that limpid they would shed' and 'wisps of day when the curtain closes. Of itself by slow millimetres'.[10] Fragments from *Lessness* were inscribed on the General Post Office on O'Connell Street, a landmark famous for its role in the 1916 Easter rebellion, for example: 'Figment light never was but grey air timeless no sound' and 'no sound no stir as grey sky mirrored'.[11] The words materialised brightly against the dark buildings, even if oddly de-contextualised from the rest of the text.

Holzer's work had several functions. When set against the programme as a whole, it fulfilled one of Colgan's ambitions as Chair of the centenary festival committee. There was an intent with this work to create new audiences, to, as he put it – somewhat paternalistically – 'understand and not to be afraid' of Beckett (*The Irish Times*, 2006). Holzer's work made these audiences in a literal way, as people on the streets became unwitting readers of Beckett's work. The other function was to do with Ireland's commemoration of its authors: Colgan reiterated the aims of the earlier festivals as a chance 'for Ireland to just stake its claim and say we have given birth to great literary giants and when their centenary comes along we should celebrate them' (*The Irish Times*, 2006). Holzer's work, coming within that broader tapestry of a city staging Beckett and his face, provided a visual confirmation of Beckett's place in the city, even if a closer reading might show this as somewhat undercut by the content of the texts chosen. There does not appear to have been a particular strategy to have landmarks and text reflect each other in any coherent way; the choice to cite Beckett's more abstract later prose as opposed to the more locatable and Dublin-centred early work is indicative of this. This resulted in a satisfying Beckettian subtlety – the equation of place and person remained incomplete, as did the text, fading at the edges, stretching into unreadability over roads or water. Yet under the aegis of this centenary, which had such a strong commitment to recognising the visual within Beckett's work (a symposium devoted to the topic at TCD was embedded in the programme), it formed a potent if ephemeral visual concision of place and writing, of the relationship between literary and urban spatiality. The confluence of textuality and public space provided a rather pointed commentary also on the city's literary tourism industry, signalling the role that festivalised commemorations can play in establishing – and re-establishing – authorial connection to place.

These two festivals represent specific ways of constructing (or reconstructing) an authorial relationship with place. Moreover, they demonstrate a particular and highly visual configuration of the perception of Beckett's

---

[10] https://projects.jennyholzer.com/projections/dublin-2006/gallery#5.

[11] https://projects.jennyholzer.com/projections/dublin-2006/gallery#10.

place in Irish culture. As noted, it might be an overstatement to suggest that Beckett was ignored within Irish culture prior to the late 1980s, as Foster's comments on the repatriation of exiles would imply. What is evident though, both from scholarship on the Irish Beckett and from discussions of recuperation and reclamation of Irish writers, is a growing discomfort with political and commercial uses of culture. As noted above, festivals were emerging at this time in Ireland and internationally as vehicles for the implementation of culture for other projects, such as place-marketing, city-branding and so forth. They are increasingly seen less as neutral sites upon which culture flourishes but as ideological apparatuses through which inequalities of class, access, and education might be perpetuated.[12] Festivalisation was also the most visible means by which versions of the nation and national belonging might be articulated. It might be suggested therefore that it is less the content of the connection between Beckett and Ireland that troubled commentators, and more so the growing critical awareness of the emergence of cultures of festivalisation, with the sorts of cultural capitalisation and commodification that these bring. The kinds of recuperation through festivals, summer schools and other commemorations that Foster and (later) Singleton critique might be read as symptoms and signs, harbingers of the ways that culture might be used to paint over societal cracks, belying inequality and precarity. Beckett's disaffection for Ireland is merely one early example of a disjuncture sutured over by festival practices, even as his work becomes one of the means by which a version of Irish national culture is produced.

To address this idea more deeply, it might be observed that Beckett, among Dublin's other literary giants, not only becomes part of the city's visual fabric through festivals but also becomes a means by which city itself is staged and produced. Festivals today play a vital role in shaping cities, frequently for the tourist gaze. Lamenting what he sees as the 'museumification' of cities, d'Eramo suggests that festival towns 'are given World Heritage status because they are already theatrical backdrops, picturesque still lifes' and the 'theatrical or musical performances the label attracts can afford them a semblance of vitality' (2021, 97). The festival, not unlike the tourist marketer, directs the scene, staging the city or landscape via an alternative cartographic mapping of a particular place, offering a way of routing bodies through urban space that fosters the consumption of cultural objects and experiences. The cartographic re-mapping of a space through the festival not only directs the visitor around the

---

[12] For more on festivalisation and its relationship with spatial and economic inequality, see the work of cultural geographers such as Sharon Zukin (1995), as well as David Harvey (for instance Harvey, 1989). These theoretical works on space and spatial practices are heavily influenced by theorists such as Henri Lefebvre (see Lefebvre, 1991).

city, demarcating cultural institutions for entertainment and social gathering, but it also materialises the city in novel ways for visitor and dweller alike, remapping the city along the lines of cultural production rather than historic, civic, political, or capitalist endeavour alone, though these of course can and do interweave. This alternative festival mapping has much in common with tourist mapping, which presumes non-knowledge of the space and produces a version of the city heavily invested in leisure, entertainment, and experiences; it becomes a city or town, in other words, staging itself for the gaze of the visitor (the UNESCO Creative Cities network might exemplify this confluence effectively, https://en.unesco.org/creative-cities/). For d'Eramo, the results of this process have seen cities in recent times cross the 'threshold' into becoming a 'tourist city', in which, rather than tourists using services and provisions designed for residents, 'residents are forced to use services and provisions designed for tourists' (2021, 78). We can see how the 1991 Festival offers itself as a signature event for the City of Culture celebrations that year, while the 2006 Centenary spills over institutional boundaries to move out into the streets, literally making audiences for Beckett's work out of passers-by.

Just as the strolling figure of the *flâneur* of the nineteenth century provided an important symbolic entity for Walter Benjamin, in which the city (Paris) becomes the staging ground for capitalist modernity and promenade-as-consumption (2002, 10), the tourist of the latter part of the twentieth-century signals the leisure-as-consumption of late capitalism. Contemporary tourist practices are grounded in traditional interactions with the marketplace, such as hotel stays, tours, souvenir shopping, for instance, but also in emergent, novel versions of consumption, in which the experience itself is what is being purchased and consumed. It is no accident that one of the major texts on what is known as the 'experience economy' (Pine and Gilmore, 2011) is structured around theatrical metaphors, with chapters such as 'Work is Theatre', 'Now Act Your Part'. Tourism marketing stages the city, in a sense, and the tourist is frequently an immersed participant in its 'drama'. In fact, it is in this staging, in all its constructedness, that the tourist site becomes demarcated as 'authentic' for the tourist (MacCannell, 1999 [1976], 100–2). In their preface, Pine and Gilmore emphasize that 'Goods and services are no longer enough. ... To realize revenue growth and increased employments, the staging of experiences must be pursued as a distinct form of economic output' (2011, ix). While we might view Pine and Gilmore's optimism at the 'opportunity' this offers for 'value creation in staging experience' with dismay, given the state of the global economic inequalities and looming climate catastrophes, they provide a pithy description at least of consumption habits of the twenty-first century – habits festival cultures of the global north have contributed to in significant ways. What we might conclude from this is that even as the city of Dublin staged Beckett in 1991 and in 2006 (and continually as a Dublin icon), Beckett, along with other literary figures, assists in 'staging' the city.

The implications of this mobilisation of art are significant. For MacCannell, the ideological expansion of modern society is intimately linked to modern mass leisure, especially to international tourism and sightseeing (1999 [1976], 3). In his 1970s text, he sees the tourist as 'one of the best models available for modern-man[*sic*]-in-general', writing that our 'first apprehension of modern civilization, it seems to me, emerges in the mind of the tourist' (1). The tourist gaze functions as a sort of inoculation against the past and our relation to nature, with the effect of making 'the present more unified against the past, more in control of nature, less a product of history' (83). Specific to the Irish context is the 'theme-parkification' of culture and heritage in Ireland, in which history itself is 'retailed and retold' for the tourist market (McCarthy, 2005, 40). While contestations over the Irish historical narrative are nothing new, for Foster, this suggests that history can be easily 'arranged into presentations, or pantheons, or waxwork shows, or interpretative centres' (2001, 24). As Emer Sheerin has observed, Irish tourism trades upon 'a very selective and exclusively aesthetic representation of Ireland', in which there is a constant attempt to discover what is 'visually appealing and exotic' while ignoring poverty and conflict (quoted in Smyth, 2001, 31). Tourism itself in Ireland has also been historically marked by a connection with imperialism, as Gerry Smyth shows (2001, 27–9). While contestations over space characterise the Irish story under colonialism, spatial organisation in the latter part of the twentieth century – whether that involves cartographic practices for the tourist gaze (and dollar) or through the development of specific routes and centres – plays the most recent role in this process. The festival necessarily becomes implicated in this and cannot be seen as external to these concerns.

Individual artworks, even when presented within festivals, may of course defy this. Contrast the festival discourses addressed here with Sarah Jane Scaife's work and the ways that she makes Beckett's art of poverty speak to actual poverty. Her work has addressed the social ills generated by the 2008 financial crash and the sorts of government policies that further disadvantaged people and worsened homelessness in Dublin and elsewhere, and an historic neglect of inner-city spaces and their communities in the rush to gentrify. Even at the height of the economic boom years known as the Celtic Tiger (1994–2007), the unevenness of development and distribution of wealth was apparent; with the 2008 crash, these inequalities only worsened. For instance, the year Scaife sited *Act Without Words II* and *Rough for Theatre I* in an inner-city

Dublin car park, homelessness charity Focus Ireland saw a 25 per cent increase in people needing assistance (Focus Ireland, 2013; Kennedy, 2013). The siting of these plays allowed them to speak readily to that social and political context. 2013 is also the year that a new Irish navy ship was named after Beckett (there is a Yeats and Joyce too). These gestures, along with calling the latest Liffey bridge opened in 2009 after the author, count as an appropriation of cultural goods for ends never intended (although it might be suggested that naming the Irish navy warships after poets and writers may be in keeping with a small island's pacifist image). They represent the use of cultural goods and figures as cement for an ideological gloss that might belie a less palatable reality.

There is a link between festivalisation and gentrification, and the contemporary cultural sector continues to grapple with questions of equality and access;[13] festivals often become a means of urban branding and part of urban regeneration projects which have frequently more to do with attracting tourism and business than with developing facilities for local populations, as Philip Boland's critique of the European Capital of Culture phenomenon shows with clarity (Boland, 2010). While festivals cannot be accused of creating the conditions for such appropriations to occur, since the 1990s they can be seen as one of the vectors by which art is connected both to the cultural economy and to wider ideological forces. Broadly, these Beckett-related commemorative events offer a glimpse into some of the public uses of art and artistic legacy, with the most pointed example of this lying in the festivals' participation in staging the city for the tourist gaze.

5 Tourist Epistemologies: The Beckett Bus

While tourism and leisure are quintessentially modern phenomena, the phenomenon of travel for knowledge is an old one. Andrea Wilson Nightingale considers how the very concept of knowledge ('theory') in fourth-century BCE Greece was linked to and emerged out of the practice of travelling abroad and watching spectacles at religious festivals (2004, 35). Such travellers were known as *theoroi* and their journeys included pilgrimages to religious festivals, visits to oracular centres, journeys abroad for the sake of learning; common among these was the sense of a journey taken for the sake of some form of learning. *Theoroi* were frequently civic ambassadors travelling on behalf of

---

[13] The trajectory of Richard Florida's work illustrates this. In the early 2000s he advocated for culture as a means of urban regeneration (see *The Rise of the Creative Class*, 2004, for instance) and was highly influential on cultural policy in some US, UK, Irish, and European contexts. He later admitted in *The New Urban Crisis* (2017) that creative industry policies deriving from his propositions have significantly increased inequality through gentrification.

their city; they could also be individual travellers. This presents a compelling historical connection between epistemology, travel, and festival. A similar equation of travel and knowledge can be found in the beginnings of tourism in early modernity. The Grand Tours were a form of early tourism in the seventeenth to nineteenth centuries that signaled the completion of an English gentleman's education and involved travel to Paris, as well as Italy or Spain, especially to the great cities of the Renaissance. While travel and leisure in the twentieth century became increasingly democratised, we can see how some of the features of more ancient festival forms shape festivals today; these include the visiting of outsiders to a place and the idea of travel for culture as inherently enriching and valuable.

The uses of space by the Gate Beckett and HDE festivals provide compelling comparison: while the Gate worked with and within the frames of existing and renowned urban cultural institutions, the HDE has at its disposal far more limited cultural institutions with a much smaller urban city (town, really) and because of this expands beyond the boundaries of what would normally be considered sites for art (and in so doing makes a virtue of this necessity). Scarcity and novelty are the drivers behind the HDE's use of site. The lack of performance spaces demands a creative engagement with site and, in light of the brevity of many of Beckett's works, the HDE employs a strategy of programming journeys to and from these sites, frequently involving a bus or boat. In fact, the journey might be seen as a fundamental part of the performance-event, one which brings the landscape, the collectiveness of bus travel, and the idea of travel for the sake of knowledge or experience into play. Consideration of the spatiality of the festival demands some engagement with the bus as a medium for art, the bus being of course a behemoth of the Irish tourism industry, vehicle of the 'hordes' of tourist (they only ever come in hordes, it seems) that locals simultaneously lament and thank for their custom. In the following, I will therefore consider how bus transport mediates spatiality and spectator experience in several HDE events: the distortion of space through bus travel in Adrian Dunbar's production of *Catastrophe* in a 'secret location'; the referencing of occupation and plantation in Netia Jones's *Stirrings Still* at the Archdale Estate and, finally, the invocations of pilgrimage and sacred tourism in what I will loosely call the island events – these include dawn readings from Beckett's work, as well as a production of *Ohio Impromptu* on Devenish Island on Lough Erne.

In general, the HDE-sited performances bring attendees to places around Enniskillen that feed a tourist's eye and avoid, in festival director Seán Doran's words, 'the noise of the festival' (Doran, 2018, 153). Again, there is a touristic staging of place evident in the events. These routes have been used – particularly the boat trips to various islands on the River Erne – since the late nineteenth century and the beginnings of the emergence of democratised forms of leisure. Furthermore, one of those agendas that permeates a festival, especially one held in a rural area, is to do with the festival's capacity to enhance place as tourist attraction. As Thomas O'Reilly (O'Reilly, 2012), Chairman of Fermanagh District Council, puts it in the 2012 inaugural programme: 'By using venues in and around the island town of Enniskillen, the festival will showcase our waterways, landscape, buildings and streets as a hub for arts, culture and sport. Whether you are familiar with Enniskillen or not, you find unique events in unique places and a warm welcome to all'.[14]

O'Reilly's attitude is not uncommon when it comes to festivals, and it is enhanced in many ways by how Doran uses space: often in the open air or underground (in the Marble Arch caves), in abandoned barns, churches and other ruins (Doran, 2018). The journey to and from these places is key. While the Gate Festival was characterised by multiple billings at irregular timeslots during each day of its several-week run, HDE solves the problem of Beckett's brevity through novel uses of space – a geographic/topological solution to a theatrical problem.

HDE programming sees work spilling over boundaries: institutional ones, geographic ones in terms of the urban-rural divide, as well as the boundaries set by genre (many of the prose, radio, filmic works have been given performative outings of some sort since the festival's inception). Indeed, the setting of Enniskillen itself, a region with its own complex relation to identity is an upset to a narrowly Irish construction of the author. The relationship between Beckett and Enniskillen is more tenuous than that between the author and Dublin. There is a primary fault line in operation here, one that is somehow both articulated and blurred by the playful, festive, and decidedly non-reverential engagement of local Enniskillenites. This is a feeling that pervades the Beckett-Enniskillen connection and one not out of keeping with the work itself, work in which place itself operates in a febrile and tense manner, never straightforwardly. This 'unruly' festival therefore frames the work differently, especially in regard to the shorter works produced site-specifically (or, more aptly termed, site-sympathetically, as in performances made for similar sorts of sites; see Wilkie, 2002, 149–50). Programming a journey to and from a site of performance allows for a more complete theatrical event for the spectator – Beckett's brevity is both the demand and, as Doran puts it, 'the solution' here (2018, 152); it also allows a spectator to give full attention to a particular work, rather than having to deal with several plays running consecutively in a multiple billing.

---

[14] Programme held by the author.

For Dunbar's *Catastrophe*, spectators gathered to catch the bus in the centre of Enniskillen town. That the bus smelled slightly of its day-job ferrying high-schoolers did not detract from the experience but rather enhanced the sense of the event as authentically ad hoc. The location of the production was kept secret by the organisers and audiences were asked to maintain that secrecy for other festival-goers yet to see the production. Thinking on it now, I am reminded of several things: one, the pleasurable lull of giving over control of one's travel to an external force, a driver, a festival organiser, someone else's aesthetic-touristic vision; two, the distortion of spatiality that came with that particular event; and three, how the route we took deliberately or inadvertently exposed Northern Ireland's complicated spatiality. There is something pleasurable in having someone else take charge of one's travel and the bus affords a certain form of tourist consumption: the height of the vehicle allows one to see over hedges, into back gardens, to get a glimpse of wider terrain and organisation of the landscape. Our consumption of art at this festival becomes also a consumption of space, place, and landscape: we are *touristified* in these moments.

Furthermore, on route to this production, the bus wove in and out of the small towns that surround Enniskillen to the east. It was early August and still a significant time in the region's marching season. Unionist and Protestant communities across Northern Ireland commemorate William III's victory at the 1690 Battle of the Boyne annually on July 12 and commemorative marches by the Orange Order of Loyalists continue throughout the summer season. The Boyne victory was significant in cementing English colonial power in Ireland and for Ulster Protestants the battle ensured the survival of their plantation and a victory for their liberty, to be celebrated yearly (Bardon, 2011, 300–1); this commitment to British identity is part of what drove the partition of Ireland in 1921 and continues to be lived out by certain communities in the form of public commemorations, British (Union Jack) flags, bunting, and painted kerbstones. All of these were highly visible as we passed through the small towns, moving from pastoral farmland to a sea of Union Jacks. The journey on the bus seemed to ramble, taking in these small towns, avoiding the main road. On the return leg, we took to the main roads and found ourselves no more than ten or fifteen minutes from Enniskillen. The journey out had taken at least forty-five. There were therefore several distortions of space invoked here. There was a literal warping of space – and indeed time – through the tourist bus, and a brief immersion in the contestations over space that shapes Northern Ireland: the spatial distortion that is a political border partitioning one part of an island from the other (and which came into being during Beckett's time at school in Enniskillen), and the continual process of spatial naming and identification that comes from two sets of communities in (currently only) simmering disagreement about the nature of their belonging.

The secret location for the production was revealed to be an abandoned church, derelict but serviceable. In the wake of that journey, *Catastrophe*'s invocation of authority and the power of an authority-figure to make and remake an image necessarily called up the spectre of colonialism that haunts Northern Ireland (and indeed Ireland in general). The ways in which the spatiality of the island of Ireland has been shaped by colonial practices, including the history of imperialism that marks the tourist gaze in that region comes to the fore here. When Frank McCusker as Director turns to address 'our catastrophe' (Beckett, 1984, 300), he could be gesturing to the ruins of history that mark the site, as well as to the biopolitical management of the colonised subject. The dank and dilapidated interior of the church invokes the religious aspects of the conflict and its longer historical sweep; if Beckett's most explicitly political play finds itself obliquely referencing this particular history, that referencing is further grounded in the tourist's bus journey.

Productions at this Festival have frequently used the grounds of local 'Big House' estates, adding yet another layer to the spatial practices of the festival. Though within walking distance of the town centre, the converted stable yard at Castle Coole has been home to Anthony Gormley's *Godot*-inspired tree sculpture, while Netia Jones's *Stirrings Still* took place at Castle Archdale. These are estates that were created by the settlers or 'planters' in the region in the 1600s. Castle Coole's mansion is preserved by the National Trust and can be visited for a fee; the land around Archdale is now a camping ground and caravan park. These ruins provide not only backdrop of history for the productions that take place within them but also offer a glimpse into the flux of spatial re-organisation that occurred in the region in the 1600s, in what was the last wave of colonisation to take place in Ireland.

There is a double-edgedness to this strand of the festival work; on the one hand it offers a window onto history, but it also performs the tourism gesture of containing and packaging the past neatly, as explored above. History is implicit in the backdrop rather than the frontal focus of the work in these productions – for good reason. It remains a Beckett festival, albeit one that occupies space in unusual ways. I will return to the question of time and the weight of history as these things manifest in Beckett festivals in the next section, but for now, I want to close this commentary by thinking through another set of 'bus' journeys taken by the festival-goer, ones that take them across bodies of water rather than tarmacked roads.

Where it might be argued that, in general, the festival-goer and the tourist frequently move in step, once on the bus they positively rhyme. The bus tour is a much-derided form of tourism. There is an assumed inauthenticity to the experience, firstly to do with the sort of paternalistic guidance that is implied by having a tour company create and manage the touring schedule and, secondly, to do with the rapidity with which geographic territories are consumed. How can a tourist ever get to know anything about a place when their experience is so heavily mediated? This is an attitude as old as travel for leisure itself: John Ruskin wrote in 1849 on how the train passenger 'hardly knows the names of the principal cities through which he passes' (quoted in d'Eramo, 2021, 10–11). Locals, especially in regions heavily marketed for such forms of tourism (Ireland is a clear example), might find themselves making exactly this remark. Yet there is a specific sort of collectiveness attached to this form of tourism, one in which travel-discovery is shared among a group of strangers, and where the failure to know fully is equally distributed. The high-minded ideals of the *theoroi* collide here with these failed tourist epistemologies, even as that 'failure' is a collective, even democratic, one.

So let us do some further journeying with this festival, to land us in the evening on an island on Lough Erne, or to find us on the same island at dawn. Leaving from a jetty on the Erne that looks up the hill to Portora Royal, the boats offered a fine view of the rural shoreline, a seemingly unspoilt mass of farmland, green and dotted with houses. The production of *Ohio Impromptu* on Devenish Island indexed a number of the concerns and issues raised above. In this production, directed by Adrian Dunbar and with Frankie McCafferty as Listener and Vincent Higgins as Reader, there was a journey, the lull of the boat, the consumption of landscape and place as well as aesthetic event and, furthermore, there was in evidence the sorts of stillness and temporal slowdown that comes both with Beckett's work and with time spent in nature.

Elsewhere (McTighe, 2018b) I noted the potential for dissonance between the kinds of affect available within performances of Beckett's work and the activities of the tourist: Beckett's work tends to be grounded in absences, forgetting, and the dissolution of the image, while the tourist appears committed to the capturing of experience through visual means: the souvenir, the photograph. On the surface, they would seem to head in different directions when it comes to notions of memory, of permanence and commitments to visibility. Yet if we return to the *theoroi* of Ancient Greece, such a figuration might offer insights into what happens at the HDE, as might a critical discourse on tourism that illuminates its blind-spots, excesses and failures. To be a tourist in the late twentieth and early twenty-first centuries may have pejorative connotations, that one is a temporary visitor to a place means a lack of lived experience, an outsider, possibly a linguistic outsider, who will never comprehend the full complexity of a place or its people, one who consumes an inauthentic version of a place that caters to tourist demands.

Wilson Nightingale highlights the fact that pilgrimages to religious festivals were one of the most prominent forms of *theoria* in the classical period, as were visits to oracular centres and other journeys abroad for the sake of learning (2004, 40). While, as she notes, there has been debate over 'whether the word "*theoria*" derives from *theos* (god) or *thea* ("sight," "spectacle")', she follows scholars who see *theoria* as both spectacular and sacred event – 'sacred spectating' captures the dual significance (45). Within the spatial practices of the HDE then, there may be apparent a form of secular spirituality. The festival operates along the lines of modern tourism, with the bus and waterbus functioning as material symbols of this: ferry boats have been bringing locals to the islands for picnics since the nineteenth century (Lanigan Wood, 1990, 80). The festival also quotes a Romanticist engagement with landscape, and with ruin, at the same time as calling up a longer history of travel for religious purposes. Devenish Island was once a point along a pilgrimage route leading to Croagh Patrick in County Mayo, so when *Ohio Impromptu* was staged there in 2015, it layered together simultaneously the tourist experience and another altogether more 'spiritual' one. Part of the experience involved wandering the ruined churchyard with its fifteenth-century high cross and stepping onto the piece of land on which a monastery has stood since the sixth century. On disembarking the waterbus, the audience was divided into two groups, one group wandered the ruins, while another watched the performance inside a small cottage. The dimness and stillness of that small space, the ghostliness of performers Frankie McCafferty and Aiden Higgins, and the final lines of that play ('so sat on as though turned to stone. The sad tale a last time told'; Beckett, 1984, 288) created an alternative resonance, one that could not be reduced to consumption or tourism affect alone (McTighe, 2018b, 32). Temporality becomes all-important here: audiences were asked to occupy several different modes of temporality in engaging with this performance (and with other sorts of performances at this festival): the time of the journey to and from, the time spent as a tourist of the landscape on the waterbus and on the island, the weight of time that marks the site, weathered into the stone monuments, and, finally, the slowed down temporality of Beckett's work itself, demanding that audiences too sit on as though turned to stone.

This island event is not alone in the festival programme; frequently the festival includes dawn readings from Beckett's works which also require waterborne transportation. The musical events that are held in Enniskillen's houses of worship at various times during the festival might form a parallel here also, given the stillness demanded of the listener. All these events seem to cite a Romantic equation between aesthetics and spirituality, which is realised also in the musical strand of the programme that Doran curates, while tourist travel in particular seems to quote the spiritual travel of the pilgrimage or journey of the *theoroi*. Yet even that ethic of the festival becomes fractured and displaced in the instability created by journey and site, as various forms of failure and failed epistemologies emerge within its structure. In their 'dialogue' on Enniskillen, O'Connell and Johnson (2014) ponder if in fact site trumped production values on some occasions. Johnson recounts his experience of the dawn readings as 'magical' yet not without flaws:

> Adrian Dunbar, both a local and a professional actor, pulled out the text of *Stirrings Still* from his jeans, and stood and read it, with a 'classically' Beckettian tonal reverence entirely distant from the free context that the location had established. It was not easy to hear, not easy to understand, and quite surprising, given the quality of a festival that was also programming Robert Wilson, that it was not memorized, not embodied, nor apparently substantially rehearsed. (2014, online)

The climate presents as a further 'character' in this festival. Sited events frequently have to be cancelled or relocated due to the inclement weather of the island. In 2022 alone, a revival of the *Walking for Waiting for Godot* planned to take place at the border on Cuilcagh Mountain had to be relocated to Portora Hall, for instance, as did a production of *Not I* planned for underground in the Marble Arch Caves. The festival's short history is littered with such instances, adding further to its unruly and ad hoc qualities.

Although not a flaw of these events necessarily, one further notable feature of the festival bus journeys is the number of people I observed falling asleep on the way to and from the performances, lulled by the motion of the bus. This sanctioned relinquishing of consciousness is exactly the opposite of what is normally required of a theatre audience. It exemplifies the failed epistemology of the spectator-tourist in the most literal sense. Fraying at the edges, therefore, is a phrase that perhaps best captures the spatiality of this festival, in terms of its unruliness relative to site and genre, to the knowledges of place that are produced (or not, on rainy days), but also to the question of temporality that the next section will address. It is here that Beckett's work and festival time and space rhyme, in the peripheral given centrality, in the time we spend at the frayed internal edges of an island and with the unspooling internal edge of a body of work such as Beckett's. The question remains if we return any the wiser from this holiday at the edge, at this festival of ruins. To pursue that thought, I turn now to the construction of time within the festival event.

6 Festival Time: Carnivals of Ruin

The festival form is a unique means of manipulating cultural time and perhaps even interrupting or disrupting certain normative modes of temporal progression. Festivals have their own peculiar relation to time and temporal organisation, commonly seen as grounded in the temporary suspension of the everyday. This provides a 'temporary liberation from the prevailing truth and from the established order' in Mikhail Bakhtin's words (1984 [1965], 10), an inversion of the normative patterns of daily social life (Falassi, 1987, 3), and a temporary dismantling of the hierarchies of repression and structures of shame in Victor Turner's understanding of Carnival (1987, 88– 9). While these festival temporalities are structured by their endpoint, which involves the normative return to the everyday, the quotidian or the workday, and means they risk being the holiday that makes normal time bearable (Stallybrass & White, 1986, 13–14), the temporalities they construct are compelling. The Beckett festivals I am exploring here each construct their own variations of both festival and Beckettian temporalities. Colgan's programming of the 1991 festival organises Beckettian temporality and audience experience through institutional time, while time interweaves with site and with travel at the HDE. Each festival constructs 'Beckett-time' out of the normative fabric of social and cultural time.

Beckett's theatre makes very specific demands on those who perform it and on those who watch it. Part of this demand is grounded in temporality. There is a deliberate slowness to many of Beckett's works, a fragmentation to the story, and a lack of narrative resolution, such that his theatre does not provide the things that we so often go to the theatre for: a forward-moving story, a coherence of beginning, middle and end – among the core elements of drama that Aristotle describes in *Poetics* (2001, 6–7) – and a sense that when one comes to the end of the show that some resolution or recognition has been reached. As Rodney Sharkey has put it succinctly, Beckett's syntax is 'calibrated to a spatio-temporality that eschews teleology. In Beckett's enclosed proxemics, objective understanding of phenomena is impossible. His is a deliberately myopic vision shorn of past and blind to future' (2021, 10). In this world, embodied immediacy replaces teleology. Bodies move slowly . . ., as with the character A in the mime *Act Without Words II*, who is 'slow, awkward, absent' (Beckett, 1984, 49). Beckett's work is populated by figures whose bodies cannot move in time. Beckett's theatre asks similar things of its audiences. It is no accident that early audiences were bemused by *Waiting for Godot*; it is a play that makes us squirm in our seats with unsatisfied anticipation for something, anything, to happen. Yet that happening never arrives, but rather we are witnesses to two indigents filling the time with a banter that barely covers despair. Time elongates in performances of this play; we are frequently aware of its passing, just as Vladimir and Estragon are, as they reflect on their interaction with Pozzo and Lucky:

Vladimir: That passed the time.
Estragon: It would have passed in any case.
Vladimir: Yes, but not so rapidly (Beckett, 1993, 44).

In the course of this play we become as frustrated as the characters on stage, caught between the desire for something to happen and the desire – for some – to leave their seat for a gin at the bar. Our social world runs at a particular pace, and we are attuned to its conditions: the pace of walking in the street, the time it takes to get to work, the time spent on various tasks, the length of time spent on leisure, including theatre – this temporal order sits around us, invisible and structuring our experience. It is only when that order is disturbed, by, for example, going to see a Beckett play, or when it becomes impossible for our bodies to keep up, perhaps because of disability, that it becomes apparent at all. The great revelation of *Godot* is not whether or not the titular character ever makes an appearance; it is rather that we might see with clarity the temporal system that surrounds us and structures our expectations at every turn, pushes our bodies into certain types of motion and, frequently, punishes us when we cannot obey its logic; the latter is especially felt by those who live with disabilities.[15]

Beckett's theatre therefore has the capacity to make audiences hyperaware of time. Within the content of the work, there is frequently an alteration to the normative progression of theatrical time, with the linear arc of dramatic plot suspended, fragmented, or circling back on itself. The plays, especially the later drama, are of a minimalist brevity that is difficult to fit within the temporal frame of what counts as a night at the theatre. A play's length is itself bound to somewhat arbitrary conventions of what constitutes value in exchange for the price of a ticket, and in Beckett we see this shortened, slowed, stilled even. As Carl Lavery has argued, Beckett creates a sort of 'theatre garden' in which perception is slowed to the point

> where things and experiences that ordinarily go unnoticed are allowed to impress themselves upon us. In the process, we are weathered in the same way as the three anonymous characters that are trapped in the urns in *Play* (1963). We, too, have been enfolded in the temporal fabric of the work, attuned to a time of 'dis-appointment' that is always too slow or too late for consciousness. (2018, 19)

Lavery's article connects Beckett's 'sculpting of time' to an experimental strand of twentieth-century performance: 'Whereas dramatic theatre always seeks to

---

[15] As Ellen Samuels eloquently puts it: 'we who occupy the bodies of crip time know that we are never linear, and we rage silently – or not so silently – at the calm straightforwardness of those who live in the sheltered space of normative time' (2017).

deny its own immersion in time, to transcend the present by investing in narratives that would entertain us and so make us forget our painful grounding in the temporal, Beckett prefers to glue us to the present, allowing us to feel the passage of time itself in our bodies.' (2018, 23)

The effect of this on the spectator is hard to quantify, but we can surmise, as Lavery does, what happens when one finds oneself responding to the demands of this art: 'We are enervated and irritated: the performance resists; it produces friction and retains its autonomy. We are unable to dominate it. It escapes our desire to petrify it into meaning, to hold it in our gaze' (23). We find ourselves asked to 'tune accordingly', as the voice of *Ghost Trio* commands (Beckett, 1984, 248). Beckett time does not cater to normative models of temporality nor the teleology of the theatrical event, nor does it correspond with the illusion of fictional time on stage. Beckett's work therefore presents challenges for the maker and spectator of theatre in terms of its demanding temporality.

It also challenges the festival producer: how are these short works, often characterised by a non-dramatic stillness, to be programmed? How are they to be packaged in such a way that they are both compelling for the viewer while also maintaining the integrity of the text, in line with the management by the Estate since the author's death? With the Estate's proscriptions one factor and the temporality of the works another, looking at the history of Beckett's work in performance it is clear that one of the solutions offered to such 'problems' both within and outside of festival contexts is the practice of multiple billing. Such arrangements fill out an evening's theatre to a conventional length. This approach was taken by Lisa Dwan in her 2014 international touring 'trilogy' of *Footfalls*, *Not I*, *Rockaby*, for instance; it becomes a way of reading the work also and is not always only to do with marketing. Dwan's production, like Scaife's 2015 Dublin event 'The Women Speak', illuminated a particular thread in Beckett's writing around gender and visibility and, through the conjunction of these works, performed a gendered reading through programming as well as staging. This comes with its own problems however: for the spectator, the consecutive presentation of quite different works sometimes means that they are not 'digested' in full. Many of the shorter works require a slowed down form of engagement and reflection, so that to rattle through, curtain up–curtain down can diminish their effect. Scaife solved this problem effectively by deploying a promenade approach, moving audiences from room to room in her chosen site. By contrast, proscenium arch stage productions can do little but move from one play to another in quite short a space of time. Regardless of site and context, while the text remains unchanged, the frame of presentation of course influences. This was highly apparent in

Scaife's feminist and politicised billing, in which both site and programming meant the works spoke directly to Ireland's history of misogynist cultural practices of institutionalising women who had become pregnant out of wed-lock. That the frame of the programme becomes visible in these moments can be connected with the discussion of festivals that I am setting out here. Beckett festivals have made frequent use of multiple billings, none more so than the Gate in 1991.

The Gate's 1991 festival dealt with the temporality of the work through establishing a specific temporal logic in which to house it. The programme had a tripartite structure: three weeks of events, three institutions. While it organised the shorter works into multiple billings, the festival played with slightly less conventional timeslots throughout. The longer dramatic works were programmed at the 20.15 timeslot, while the shorter plays took place at lunchtime or later in the evening at a 23.15 timeslot. Raidió Teilifís Éireann broadcast Barry McGovern reading from *Malone Dies* and added the televi-sion plays into late evening slots, while the radio plays were broadcast in 16.00 and 20.15 slots. This organisation of the temporality of these texts into, in Colgan's words, an *Event*, is a compelling one. We see Beckettian time meet media time, by which I mean the temporality of theatrical, televisual or radio conventions. The programming on radio and television is indicative of the status of Beckett's works relative to those, more popular, media, while the theatre programming expands the normal hours of theatri-cal convention quite a bit. This careful framing is one way for the rupture of temporality contained within Beckett's work to be experienced by audi-ences. Taken altogether, the programme offered a feast of Beckettian work, carefully framed through medium-specific temporalities.

Regarding the organisation of the theatre works, Gerry Colgan (1991) notes that the first offering of the festival being *Waiting for Godot* was virtually mandatory and that it was 'critical that it should set the tone and a pace for the rest'. Of particular note was the success of the shorter works:

> The success of the short plays, presented in groups of three in mid-day and late-night productions, was in its way the most extraordinary of all. Packed houses came to soak up the atmosphere, the essence of these apparently recondite works, because they had come to know that Beckett is part experience, part sensation, and perhaps least of all an intellectual chal-lenge. (Colgan, 1991, 8)

'The festival', for Matt Wolf, 'granted a rare and educative opportunity to see double and triple bills of works which couldn't help but comment on one another' (1991). Reviewers tended to agree both on the success of the strategies deployed – these include marketing as well as programming – as well as on the navigation of that distance that had characterised Beckett's personal relationship with Ireland.

For Colgan, the arrangement of Beckett's work in this way was what he termed 'eventing': a combination of homage, strategic programming, smart marketing, as well as the generation of an aura around the work:

> I don't think audiences will sit down for two hours anymore unless you give them a reward. And the reward you give them is by telling them that they have been to an *Event*. When you *Event* something you've a much better chance of getting them to sit through even five hours. They can get together, make it to a communal event, have supper and sandwiches and they're all happy doing the marathon. I had no difficulty in getting people to come and see the Becketts in 1991 in London and in New York.
>
> (Colgan, 2001, 82; emphasis in original)

Unworried, as Clare comments, by 'criticisms of those who suggest that "festivalization" has resulted in the increased "commodification" of culture' (Clare, 2016, 47), Colgan's strategy reflects a wider trend among theatre producers that Patrick Lonergan notes, providing an opportunity to see a unique or limited, and therefore scarce, event (Lonergan, 2008, 217). It also reflects, as already mentioned in this section, the Gate's status as an only partially publicly funded theatre, which Colgan has always argued has meant that the theatre needed to be cannier when it comes to the box office. This canniness manifested in strategies like limited runs, celebrity casting, as well as, in regard to the Beckett festivals, the interweaving of culturally nationalist projects. In his 'eventing', Colgan was establishing the value of Beckett for Irish audiences, a gesture that was further fomented by the Lincoln Centre tour in 1996: Lonergan notes the impact that international touring of Irish theatre work in the 1990s had on national reception – positive reviews overseas boosted confidence in the work at home (2008, 54–5).

Colgan is also implicitly drawing an equation between Beckett's work and the festival form. This process of eventing often also requires a remaking of authorial image or of the understanding of the work – note the ways in which audiences are caused to understand Beckett differently in Gerry Colgan's estimation – and with this comes a softening of some of the more uncomfortable and difficult elements of the work itself. This affective shift is clearly processed through the 1991 festival and further confirmed by the time of the 2006 centenary and the sophisticated literary tourist practices and narratives that have come to shape the city by that time. Connecting these two observations, we might think of these Beckett events as 'feasts', with all the maximalism that this implies. Even if the staged works respectfully retain their minimalist

Beckettian credentials, the festival form, or at least Michael Colgan's vision of it, supplies the energy and the concentrated consumption of the feast. The question of the cost of this strategy to audiences' understanding of and absorption in the work remains unanswered.

With its use of site and travel, Netia Jones's staging of *Stirrings Still* exemplifies the spatial practices of the HDE and offers further ways of thinking through the temporalities afforded by this festival, and by festivals in general. It provides a perspective on how Beckettian temporal modes interweave with festival time. Like *Ohio Impromptu* on the island, this production embodies many aspects of the HDE's aesthetics: it is site-sympathetic, with audiences bussed to and from a secret location, and it engineers a complex layering of past and present, tourist time and aesthetic time, the time of travel and the time of still contemplation.

This production was sited in an abandoned outbuilding on the grounds of the Archdale Estate. Audiences taking the bus from Enniskillen found themselves engaging with place and landscape in the way I have described in the preceding section and, arriving at the location, were ushered to the second floor of a ruinous barn, where McElhinney was seated in side-profile, recessed through a narrow doorway. Light illuminated his face and created the impression of a window behind him. The design reflected the details of this short prose text: 'light of a kind came then from the one high window' (Beckett, 2015, 11). In front and to the left of the doorway, the wall formed a canvas which Jones used to project, variously, the image of the window, a live feed of McElhinney, and, when he emerged to stand facing the wall, dynamic monochrome footage appeared of clouds and grass ('he moved on through the long hoar grass'; Beckett, 2015, 19), and floated across his back; these were broken only by the dark shadow of his figure, in hat and greatcoat, against the wall. The digital imaging rendered him both present and absent, both ghostly projection and material entity. The ruined building with the actor recessed within it illuminated the intense interiority of that text and, perhaps most importantly, the proximity to decay lent the piece a particular atmosphere, one that did not make sense of the text but rather enfolded the audience within its haunted affect of finitude. The journey to the site became also a journey through several different modes of temporality.

The bus ride took almost an hour and was one of tension between the forward motion of the moving bus and the stillness of my body, the moving towards an aesthetic object and comparative stillness of the surrounding fields. In my memory of the performance, it seems as if it lasted only a very short time, it exists for me now as a series of potent images, yet I remember also that in this small, dilapidated space, time seemed to elongate, my perception was arrested in the moment by both the still sparseness of the words and the stark and austere beauty of the images.[16] Each stage of the journey that the audience underwent carried a temporality all of its own: there was the festival time, navigable via the festival programme, the 'tourist time' of the bus journey, the arrival at a ruin with the weight of history's presence, and of course the Beckettian time of the performance itself. Outside the ruin, a gramophone played the music of Schubert, cueing both the musical threads that interweave the festival and the era of nineteenth-century romanticism that fluoresces with frequency in Beckett's work. Both the object of the gramophone and the barn itself appear out of time, their presence an anachronism, a further jolt to any notion of linear temporality. These dregs of history, in a place still heavily marked by the spatial organisation of the past, index this festival's animation of the ruin.

Once seated, audiences were asked to adjust to a new temporality, that of the performance. The 'speaker' of the piece, McElhinney's voiceover, talks of time, 'so slow that only change of place to show he went' (Beckett, 2015, 12), of the strokes of a clock striking 'the hours and half-hours' (13). The journey we travelled asked us to pass through varying layers of temporality: from the bustling summer tourism of Enniskillen to that of sightseeing and landscape-absorption, to the temporality of this leftover building on its way to dereliction, to the markers of nostalgia in the gramophone, and finally to the Beckett-time of the performance, itself an even slower pace. The slow – almost still – temporality is the culmination of a question asked of the audience: can you slow down, can you be still, can you find a different form of temporality in the moment of performance? After the performance we emerged blinking into the light, a little like the figure of the narrative, 'at last out again he knew not how' (17).

The temporal journey was more affective than intellectual; what we experienced had more to do with the affect of time passing and a sense of temporal layering than with consuming cultural products. This is perhaps the point at which Beckett and festivals cohere, where the content of his oeuvre and the festival form are most legibly intertwined, in asking spectators (and perhaps artists too) to engage with forms of temporality outside the norms of daily life. That festivals suspend time is not a new idea but takes on a particular flavour within the context of late-stage and neoliberal capitalism, outside of which it is difficult to read the festivalisation of Beckett. While it might be suggested that Colgan finds the slickest way of making the Beckett feast a palatable affair for its audiences, Doran chooses to 'solve' the challenge of Beckett's brevity through the use of site and the creation of a journey, sometimes of up to an hour, between

---

[16] Productions shots, including of the ruined building, can be found on Jones's website: https://netiajones.com/project/stirrings-still/#&gid=1&pid=5.

the centre of Enniskillen and the site of the performance. Rather than sitting into pre-ordained medium-specific temporal conventions, theatre-makers like Jones are then free to create a work of shorter length than would normally be acceptable. She comments that she finds it liberating to be relieved of the pressure to work towards an arbitrary equation of time and value in theatre, in order to produce works of appropriate lengths to satisfy audiences' expectations (Jones, 2020).

One of the other challenges that theatre-makers face when adapting Beckett's prose work is that the materiality and embodied nature of theatre can close off the fluid placelessness and timelessness that permeate these texts of self-conscious interiority. While the Dublin Beckett festivals have tended to stay within the boundaries of genre, the HDE has received and commissioned a significant number of cross-medial works. Jones's work and indeed many of this festival's commissioned adaptations navigate the problems attached to materialisation and embodiment through the use of site alongside the distortion of temporality. Layering varying modes of temporality together within a single aesthetic experience and confronting audiences with an unfamiliar place (or a place made unfamiliar through performance) means that these works, of which *Stirrings Still* is an excellent example, embody both placedness and placeless-ness. They are subject to the temporal logics of journey and performance but, in the moment of their presentation, seem to slip outside of normative modes of temporality.[17] Journey and site are not the only means by which this effect comes into being, therefore, and we need to recognise that much of this is located in Beckett's writing itself. However, a festival context, as Jones herself puts it, embodies its own 'obliteration' of any normal schedule, allowing festival-goers to step out of normal time, to choose their own path through the festival offerings and perhaps suspend judgement and attend performances that they would not otherwise countenance (Jones, 2020). Site is an important additive to this festival 'time' helping to produce layered temporalities around the work as well as interweave with or even alter the work's meaning. In a sense, festival events expand the horizon of audience expectations; this was certainly the case with Michael Colgan's 'eventified' Beckett and it is especially the case with a bijoux festival such as the HDE.

When Jones articulates how the festival form allows her to experiment with time, she is saying something both pragmatic and profound: pragmatic, because

---

[17] A worthy comparison to this is Olwen Fouéré's 2015 version of *Lessness* (which premiered at the Barbican's Beckett International Season and toured to the Galway International Arts Festival in 2015, then to the Project Arts Centre, Dublin city and the Mermaid Arts Centre, Bray in 2016), which is designed to be performed in a theatre but manages to invoke a similar temporal suspension.

the festival offers space for her as a theatre-maker to create or adapt work that does not obey the temporal logic of theatre in its normative forms. She can make work that lasts a half an hour, or even less, and because that is contained with a broader frame of festival form, this work of unusual brevity can become legible and acceptable as a piece of performance. That festivals frequently have the luxury of programming work during the day and not only at night tells us much about the suspension of the chrono-normative expectations about work and leisure time. The festival form in general upends dominant temporalities therefore, in multiple ways. This is the philosophical idea that arrives alongside observations about the pragmatics of making and programming performance.

The sort of Beckett *Events* under discussion here take place outside the festival frame also: the journey-performance can take place in non-festival time, and site-specific/generic work on Beckett invokes this temporality also. This is exemplified by Scaife's work: the production of *Act Without Words II* asks the spectator to come to grips with the time of material poverty and indigence through siting the work in back alleys (Scaife, 2016; Singleton, 2016) and other depopulated urban spaces; this work has operated in and out of various festival contexts and often requires walking through urban spaces to reach the outdoor performance site. It is worth noting also that these complex festival temporalities already inhere within a significant number of avant-garde and experimental theatre practices of the twentieth century.[18] What is worth articulating here however is the almost unique confluence of Beckettian time and the space that is created for it within a Beckett-dedicated festival. The festival may not have the monopoly on the aesthetic event, but in materialising the frame of the festival, the space it creates for such things and the role it plays in the contemporary construction of space and time relative to leisure has, it is hoped, become clearer. Certainly, many analyses of festivals indicate that there is a specific organisation of temporality available within these events that offers audiences a suspension of the everyday unfolding over a period of time, rather than just one evening. When we make visible the frame of the festival itself as the means by which the artworks come into being – the bus, the journey and so on – then we start to see the form and its spatial and temporal structures exposed.

7 Conclusion: Degenerate Gatherings

Finally, I would like to pick up on a thread in that imprecise equation of Beckett and festivals that has been glimpsed at points throughout this study, that of Beckett's work relative to the communities that form in and around festivals.

---

[18] A useful account of these can be found in Hans-Thies Lehmann's *Postdramatic Theatre* (2006), in particular the 'Aspects' chapter (145–74).

Festivals, as Erika Fischer-Lichte puts it, 'create communities' (2014, 44). In this Element, I have traced the structures that organise bodies through festivals, and the spatial and temporal practices that they quote and invoke. I have examined the ways in which varying discourses of nation, of cultural value, and tourist marketing are interwoven with Beckett's work through the festival form, and I have examined how that work's temporalities may resist the smooth veneer with which festivalisation overlays reality. Community forms the final thread to tie these matters together and to signal to the further and future work that is needed in regard to the festivalised Beckett.

I commenced with the notion that when the artwork is subjected to festival temporality, it may be simultaneously subjected to the temporality of neoliberal consumption, thereby becoming another investment in the experience economy and a means of mapping spaces for patterns of consumption and leisure; many festivals which purport to be community-related are in fact simply marketing opportunities. Many festivals parachute into a place and offer little to local communities. Yet festivals may help to construct alternative spatial forms and may provide multifaceted, complex layerings of time that, regardless of the content of the festival, set leisure time against the time of work. They offer resistance to what Elizabeth Freeman names the chrono-normative, the 'use of time to organize human bodies towards maximum productivity'. For Freeman this is a 'mode of implantation, a technique by which institutional forces come to seem like somatic facts'. Importantly for this discussion, Freeman's queer reading locates the chrono-normative in the body, a means through which 'flesh is bound into socially meaningful embodiment through temporal regulation' (2010, 3). Reflecting on festivals opens space for the consideration of the ambiguous and contradictory politics of festivals, the nature of the public sphere, and how we organise bodies in and through the shared spaces of public assembly.

Festivals carry the potential to function as interruptive forces and it may be that their politics lie in the alternative temporalities they construct, as well as the ways that they open spaces and times for communal critical judgement and reflection. For Zaiontz, this potential lies in the sorts of festivals that include or emphasise public, participatory events, and that mobilise artists and audiences to imagine political alternatives to dominant ideas and structures. Connecting festivals and political protest movements allows her to think of new ways festivals can play a role in public life 'stretching beyond a single production or annual festival programme' (Zaiontz, 2020, 25). Yet festivals may also serve the ends of capitalist approaches to culture: they facilitate certain constructions of space and spatiality, assisting, as I have argued Section 4, in the staging and branding of places to serve both tourist and corporate interests. There are several different perspectives on Beckett as 'event' running throughout the festival discourses I have highlighted in this Element, and which reflect this ambiguity. Colgan's 'Eventification' may be read as marketing strategy and one solution to Beckett's artistic brevity. I have considered also how this bends Beckett time to the structures of institutional temporality and theatrical aesthetic consumption. Across the 1991 and 2006 Dublin Beckett festivals, an increasing commitment to the visual and to public artworks might on the one hand be seen as reflective of a growing understanding of the democratic and shared nature of art; it may, on the other hand, be indicative of a strengthening cohesion between public institutions and corporate entities, united by notions of 'culture' and 'creativity'. Some of the work of the HDE, specifically what we will call the sited 'journey-works', might promise greater interruption to the chrono-normative order and to the supposed productivity of neoliberal time. The HDE offers unruly temporalities, spilling over spatial boundaries and constituting a somewhat different sort of 'event', even if it too quotes tourism's spatial practices and invests in celebrity casting. A resolution to the extensive sets of tensions in operation between festivals on the one hand and Beckett on the other seems out of reach: the specularity and publicity attached to one seeming an anathema to the other. Yet this study has shown the novel interchanges that occur between Beckett's work and, variously, the spatial practices of the tourist, the carnivalesque interruption of time, and the spectacles of literary tourism and authorial commemoration. If Beckett's work can be shown to sit uneasily beside such things, then it is a productive uneasiness that can be mobilised to make visible and dissect festivalising practices and their ambiguities.

The suspension of everyday activities has the potential to engineer spaces of openness, to engender alternative modes of embodiment, and perhaps even alternative ways of perceiving and understanding the world. The suspension of the everyday is found in forms of direct political protest and action and may be detectable within individual art events themselves, but it is perhaps only within the shared spaces of festivals, as Zaiontz suggests, that the commonalities between these things become visible. Considering Beckett's work relative not only to public space but also to the public sphere, the realm of social life where public opinion is formed, as Jürgen Habermas describes it (1974, 49), demonstrates the often implicit politics attached to the presentation and programming of art. While it is difficult, if not impossible, to make broad claims about festivals, we can observe a qualitative difference in the way that they take up space and time, as compared to individual art events, performances, exhibitions, concerts and so forth, and a difference too in the invitation that is offered to the spectator to navigate their own route through the festival offerings. As noted in the introduction and drawing on Rancière, festivals play a part in the ideological determination of the seen and heard. The festival-goer might be seen, however, as an example of Rancière's emancipated spectator, defying the binary between viewing and acting that the philosopher explores (2011, 13). The festival-goer actively constructs their own path through a festival pro-gramme, organising time and their access to space in a way that is agentic and thoughtful, as gestures of doing and spectating are enmeshed. More pessimis-tically, one might counter that festivals simply maximise choice and consump-tion for the privileged few in ways that correspond to individuated neoliberal habits. However we read the situation, due caution is necessary perhaps about the liberatory possibilities attached to events that are always circumscribed or shaped by the economic and political conditions which frame them and the bodies that move through them, especially when we focus on the individual's experience of the event. We cannot forget the nature of the collective experience and its potential that runs through festivals.

Beckett, in his description of the cultural clash between the Irish and the French in St-Lô, wrote that 'their way of being we, was not our way and that our way of being they was not their way' (quoted in O'Brien, 1986, 337). Beckett festivals provide spaces and times in which we might reflect on the complicated, often divided way of doing and being 'we' and on the ethics of our actions within the shared spaces of community. In 1991, Beckett's work was performed to packed houses at the Gate. His work was also broadcast on national radio and television. These institutions directed the work towards the national community, exemplifying one way of using Beckett to construct a version of 'we'. In 2013, visitors and locals alike were confronted on their way into Enniskillen town by a large banner bearing the words of Vladimir's question from *Waiting for Godot*: 'Was I sleeping while the others suffered?' (Beckett, 1993, 82). The phrase was used as the title for the centrepiece exhibition of the HDE festival that year, documenting Beckett's time in Germany and antipathy towards the Nazis as well as his work for the French resistance. Its placement across the road presented a jarring visual example of the sort of incongruity at work between Beckett and celebration (and perhaps between Beckett and Enniskillen) on the one hand; on the other, it called up the shared ethical responsibility that lies at the heart of live spectatorship, the 'I' relative to the 'we'. Reflecting on it now, it seems there might be a provocation here to think on what it means to share space in the name of and in the wake of Beckett, and – especially – in the contested spaces of Northern Ireland. As we become subject to the interruptive temporal-ity and spatiality of Beckett in festival form, we do not do so alone. It is imperative that we consider what forms of community are constructed in and through Beckett festivals, locally and internationally, and indeed festivals in general. It is hoped that this study provides some of the coordinates through which we might commence this examination. Such festival communities are constructed over and out of the ruins that litter history, with the global pandemic of 2020–21 only the most recent fluctuation, and the ongoing ecological crisis looking set to bring yet more ruination. Beckett's art in its festival form has the capacity to demand collective engagement with, as opposed to offering an ideological veneer over, the ruinous foundations on which all our cultural edifices are constructed, festivals among them.

References

Agence France-Presse (2006), 'Dublin Comes Alive for Centenary of Beckett's Birth', 6 April.

Aristotle (2001), *Poetics: 350 BC*, trans. Samuel H. Butcher, Virginia: Virginia Tech.

Bakhtin, Mikhail (1984 [1965]), *Rabelais and His World*, trans. Helene Iswolsky, Bloomington: Indiana University Press.

Bardon, Jonathon (2011), *The Plantation of Ulster*, Dublin: Gill & Macmillan.

Battersby, Eileen (1991), 'Alarm Bells Still Ringing Out Over City of Culture', *The Irish Times*, 13 August.

Beckett, Samuel (1984), *Collected Shorter Plays*, London: Faber and Faber.

Beckett, Samuel (1987), *Proust and Three Dialogues*, London: John Calder.

Beckett, Samuel (1993), *The Theatrical Notebooks of Samuel Beckett Vol 1: Waiting for Godot*, ed. Dougald McMillan and James Knowlson, London: Faber and Faber.

Beckett, Samuel (2014), *The Letters of Samuel Beckett, Vol. III: 1957–1965*, ed. George Craig, Martha Dow Fehsenfeld, Dan Gunn and Lois More Overbeck, Cambridge: Cambridge University Press.

Beckett, Samuel (2015), *Stirrings Still*, New York: Foxrock and OR Books.

Beckett, Samuel (2016), *The Letters of Samuel Beckett, Vol. IV: 1966–1989*, ed. George Craig, Martha Dow Fehsenfeld, Dan Gunn and Lois More Overbeck, Cambridge: Cambridge University Press.

Bénard, Julie (2018), '*The Capital of the Ruins* by Samuel Beckett: Re-construction as a "Re-distribution of the Sensible"', *Études britanniques contemporaines*, 54. https://journals.openedition.org/ebc/4282#text.

Benjamin, Walter (2002), *The Arcades Project*, trans. Howard Eiland and Kevin McLaughlin, Harvard, MA: Harvard University Press.

Bennett, Andy, Jodie Taylor and Ian Woodward (2014), *The Festivalization of Culture*, Aldershot: Ashgate.

Boland, Philip (2010), '"Capital of Culture – you must be having a laugh!" Challenging the Official Rhetoric of Liverpool as the 2008 European Cultural Capital', *Social and Cultural Geography*, 11:7, pp. 627–45.

Clare, David (2016), 'The Gate Theatre's Beckett Festivals: Tensions between the Local and the Global', in Trish McTighe and David Tucker (eds.), *Staging Beckett in Ireland and Northern Ireland*, London: Bloomsbury-Methuen, pp. 39–50.

Colgan, Gerry (1991), 'Beckett Brought Home in Radiant Darkness', *The Irish Times*, 22 October, p. 8.

Colgan, Michael (2001), 'In Conversation with Jeananne Crowley', in Lillian Chambers, Ger Fitzgibbon and Eamonn Jordan (eds.), *Theatre Talk: Voices of Irish Practitioners*, Dublin: Carysfort Press, pp. 76–89.

Coopers & Lybrand (1994), *The Employment and Economic Significance of the Cultural Industries in Ireland*, Dublin: Coopers & Lybrand Corporate Finance Service.

d'Eramo, Marco (2021), *The World in a Selfie: An Inquiry into the Tourist Age*, London: Verso.

Davies, William (2017), 'A Text Become Provisional: Revisiting *The Capital of the Ruins*', *Journal of Beckett Studies*, 26:2, pp. 169–87.

de Valera, Eamon (17 March 1943), 'The Ireland that We Dreamed Of', *RTE Archives*. www.rte.ie/archives/exhibitions/eamon-de-valera/719124-address-by-mr-de-valera/.

Department of Arts, Heritage and the Gaeltacht (2016), *Dublin UNESCO City of Literature Strategic Plan 2016–2018*. www.dublincityofliterature.net/wp-content/uploads/Strategic-Plan-2016-2018.pdf.

Dettmer, Jamie (1991), 'Dublin Swoons on Beckett Binge', *The Times*, 5 October.

Dilks, Stephen (2011), *Samuel Beckett in the Literary Marketplace*, New York: Syracuse University Press.

Doran, Sean (2018), 'Interviewed by Trish McTighe', *Contemporary Theatre Review*, 28:1, pp. 150–4.

Dowd, Garin (2003), 'Karaoke Beckett, or Jeremy Irons, Mimicry and Travesty in "Ohio Impromptu" on Film', *Samuel Beckett Today/Aujourd'hui*, 13, pp. 169–82.

Duffy, Patrick J. (1997), 'Writing Ireland: Literature and Art in the Representation of Irish Place', in Brian Graham (ed.), *In Search of Ireland: A Cultural Geography*, London: Routledge, pp. 64–83.

Edinburgh Evening News (14 February 2018), 'Figures Reveal Percentage of Locals Attending Edinburgh Festivals'. www.edinburghnews.scotsman.com/whats-on/figures-reveal-percentage-locals-attending-edinburgh-festivals-588857.

Everding, Robert G. (1998), 'Planting Mulberry: A History of Shaw Festivals', *Shaw*, 18, pp. 67–91.

Falassi, Alessandro (1987), 'Festival: Definition and Morphology', in Alessandro Falassi (ed.), *Time Out of Time: Essays on the Festival*, Albuquerque: University of New Mexico Press, pp. 1–10.

Fallon, Brian (1991), 'Beckett Show at Douglas Hyde Gallery', *The Irish Times*, 15 October.

Fallon, Brian (1998), *An Age of Innocence: Irish Culture 1930–1960*, Dublin: Gill & Macmillan.

Feingold, Michael (1996), 'Irishize Unsmiling', *Village Voice*, 20 August, p. 76.

Ferriter, Diarmuid (2004), *The Transformation of Ireland 1900–2000*, London: Profile.

Festival of Britain (1952), *The Story of the Festival of Britain*, London: Festival Council.

Fischer-Lichte, Erika (2014), *The Routledge Introduction to Performance Studies*, trans. Minou Arjomand, Abingdon: Routledge.

Fitzpatrick Dean, Joan (2014), *All Dressed Up: Modern Irish Historical Pageantry*, New York: Syracuse University Press.

Florida, Richard (2004), *The Rise of the Creative Class and How it's Transforming Work, Leisure, Community and Everyday Life*, New York: Basic Civitas Books.

Florida, Richard (2017), *The New Urban Crisis*, New York: Basic Civitas Books.

Focus Ireland (2013), *Annual Report*. www.focusireland.ie/wp-content/uploads/2016/04/Focus-Ireland-Annual-Report-2013.pdf.

Foster, Robert (Roy) (1988), *Modern Ireland 1600-1972*, London: Penguin.

Foster, Robert (Roy) (2001), *The Irish Story: Telling Tales and Making It up in Ireland*, Oxford: Oxford University Press.

Freeman, Elizabeth (2010), *Time Binds: Queer Temporalities, Queer Histories*, North Carolina: Duke University Press.

Frost, Everett C. and Anna McMullan (2003), 'The Blue Angel Beckett on Film Project: Questions of Adaptation, Aesthetics and Audience in Filming Beckett's Theatrical Canon', in Linda Ben-Zvi (ed.), *Drawing on Beckett: Portraits, Performances and Cultural Contexts*, Tel Aviv: Assaph Books, pp. 215–38.

Furlong, Irene (2009), *Irish Tourism 1880–1980*, Dublin: Irish Academic Press.

Getz, Donald (2010), 'The Nature and Scope of Festival Studies', *International Journal of Event Management Research*, 5:1, pp. 1–47.

Gontarski, Stanley E. (2016), '"I think this does call for a firm stand": Beckett at the Royal Court', in David Tucker and Trish McTighe (eds.), *Staging Beckett in Great Britain*, London: Bloomsbury-Methuen, pp. 21–36.

Greene, Alexis (1996), 'The Reviews: The Beckett Festival', *Theaterweek*, 16 September, pp. 12–15.

Habermas, Jürgen (1974), 'The Public Sphere: An Encyclopaedia Article', trans. Sarah Lennox and Frank Lennox, *New German Critique*, 3, pp. 49–55.

Habicht, Werner (2001), 'Shakespeare Celebrations in Times of War', *Shakespeare Quarterly*, 52:4, pp. 441–55.

Harrington, John (1991), *The Irish Beckett*, Syracuse, NY: Syracuse University Press.

Harrington, John (2008), 'Festivals National and International: The Beckett Festival', in Nicholas Grene, Patrick Lonergan and Lillian Chambers (eds.), *Interactions: Dublin Theatre Festival 1957–2007*, Dublin: Carysfort Press, pp. 131–42.

Harris, Claudia (1992), 'The Beckett Festival', *Theatre Journal*, 44:3, pp. 405–7.

Harvey, David (1989), 'From Managerialism to Entrepreneurialism: The Transformation in Urban Governance in Late Capitalism', *Geografiska Annaler: Series B, Human Geography*, 71:1, pp. 3–17.

Harvie, Jen (2003), 'Cultural Effects of the Edinburgh International Festival: Elitism, Identities, Industries', *Contemporary Theatre Review*, 13:4, pp. 12–26.

Hauptfleisch, Temple, Shulamith Lev-Aladgem, Jacqueline Martin, Willmar Sauter and Henri Schoenmakers, eds. (2007), *Festivalising! Theatrical Events, Politics and Culture*, Leiden: Brill.

Horkheimer, Max and Theodor W. Adorno (2002), *Dialectic of Enlightenment*, trans. Edmund Jephcott, ed. Gunzelin Schmid Noeri, California: Stanford University Press.

The Irish Times (2006), 'Worldwide Plans for Beckett Centenary Unveiled', 28 February. www.irishtimes.com/news/worldwide-plans-for-beckett-centenary-unveiled-1.773613.

Johnson, Nicholas (2017), 'Keynote Address at *Beckett, Ireland and the Biographical Festival: A Symposium*', Metropolitan Arts Centre, Belfast, 17–18 November.

Johnson, Nicholas (2021), 'Coda: Viral Beckett', in Galina Kiryushina, Einat Adar and Mark Nixon (eds.), *Samuel Beckett and Technology*, Edinburgh: Edinburgh University Press, pp. 255–62.

Johnson, Nuala (2004), 'Fictional Journeys: Paper Landscapes, Tourist Trails and Dublin's Literary Texts', *Social & Cultural Geography*, 5:1, pp. 91–107.

Jones, Netia (2020), unpublished interview with Trish McTighe, 10 May.

Kahn, Coppèlia (2001), 'Remembering Shakespeare Imperially: The 1916 Tercentenary', *Shakespeare Quarterly*, 52:4, pp. 456–78.

Keenan, Siobhan and Dominic Shellard, eds. (2016), *Shakespeare's Cultural Capital: His Economic Impact from the Sixteenth to the Twenty-First Century*, Basingstoke: Palgrave Macmillan.

Kennedy, Seán (2009), 'Samuel Beckett's Reception in Ireland', in Mark Nixon and Mathew Feldman (eds.), *The International Reception of Samuel Beckett*, London: Continuum, pp. 55–74.

Kennedy, Sr Stanislaus (2013), 'There is an Urgent Need to Tackle Family Homelessness; Five Children are Becoming Homeless in Dublin Every Week, and This is Unacceptable', *The Irish Times*, 18 December, p. 16.

Kilroy, Thomas (2013), 'A Memoir of the 1950s', in Gerald Dawe, Darryl Jones and Nora Pelizzari (eds.), *Beautiful Strangers: Ireland and the World of the 1950s*, Bern: Peter Lang, pp. 7–20.

Kissel, Howard (1996), 'Godot Worth Waiting For', *Daily News*, 1 August.

Knowles, Ric, (2020a), 'Indigenous Festivals', in Ric Knowles (ed.), *The Cambridge Companion to International Theatre Festivals*, Cambridge: Cambridge University Press, pp. 70–84.

Knowles, Ric, (2020b), 'Introduction', in Ric Knowles (ed.), *The Cambridge Companion to International Theatre Festivals*, Cambridge: Cambridge University Press, pp. 1–12.

Knowlson, James (1996), *Damned to Fame: The Life of Samuel Beckett*, London: Bloomsbury.

Lanigan Wood, Helen (1990), *Enniskillen: Historic Images of an Island Town*, Belfast: Friar's Bush.

Lavery, Carl (2018), 'Ecology in Beckett's Theatre Garden: Or How to Cultivate the Oikos', *Contemporary Theatre Review*, 28:1, pp. 10–26.

Lefebvre, Henri (1991), *The Production of Space*, trans. Donald Nicholson-Smith, Oxford: Blackwell.

Lehmann, Hans-Thies (2006), *Postdramatic Theatre*, trans. Karen Jürs-Munby, London: Routledge.

Lloyd, David (2010), 'Frames of *Referrance*: Samuel Beckett as an Irish Question', in Seán Kennedy (ed.), *Beckett and Ireland*, Cambridge: Cambridge University Press, pp. 31–55.

Lonergan, Patrick (2008), *Theatre and Globalization: Irish Drama in the Celtic Tiger Era*, Basingstoke: Palgrave Macmillan.

MacCannell, Dean (1999 [1976]), *The Tourist: A New Theory of the Leisure Class*, Berkeley: University of California Press.

Maprayil, Ros (2018), 'Review of *Purgatorio: Walking for Waiting for Godot*, UNESCO Global Geopark, Enniskillen, Northern Ireland. Happy Days International Enniskillen Beckett Festival', *The Beckett Circle*, Autumn.

Marshall, Colin (2017), '"Try Again. Fail Again. Fail Better": How Samuel Beckett Created the Unlikely Mantra That Inspires Entrepreneurs', *Open Culture*, 7 December. www.openculture.com/2017/12/try-again-fail-again-fail-better-how-samuel-beckett-created-the-unlikely-mantra-that-inspires-entrepreneurs-today.html.

McCarthy, Mark (2005), 'Historico-Geographical Explorations of Ireland's Heritages: Towards a Critical Understanding of Nature of Memory and Identity', in Mark McCarthy (ed.), *Ireland's Heritages: Critical Perspectives on Memory and Identity*, Aldershot: Ashgate, pp. 3–51.

McDonald, Rónán (2009), 'Groves of Blarney: Beckett's Academic Reception in Ireland', *Nordic Irish Studies*, 8:1, pp. 29–45.

McFrederick, Matthew (2016), 'Staging Beckett: A Production History of Samuel Beckett's Drama in London (1955–2010)', unpublished doctoral thesis submitted to the University of Reading.

McMullan, Anna (1993), *Theatre on Trial: Samuel Beckett's Later Drama*, London: Routledge.

McMullan, Anna (2004), 'Irish/Postcolonial Beckett', in Lois Oppenheim (ed.), *Palgrave Advances in Samuel Beckett Studies*, Basingstoke: Palgrave Macmillan, pp. 89–109.

McTighe, Trish (2018a), '"Be again, be again": The Gate's Beckett Country', in David Clare, Des Lally and Patrick Lonergan (eds.), *The Gate Theatre, Dublin: Inspiration and Craft*, Dublin: Carysfort Press, pp. 299–314.

McTighe, Trish (2018b), 'In Caves, in Ruins: Place as Archive at the Happy Days International Beckett Festival', *Contemporary Theatre Review*, 28:1, pp. 27–38.

Meenan, James (1970), *The Irish Economy Since 1922*, Liverpool: Liverpool University Press.

Moran, James (2016), *Shrinking Violets: A Field Guide to Shyness*, London: Profile.

Morash, Christopher (2002), *A History of Irish Theatre, 1601–2000*, Cambridge: Cambridge University Press.

Murray, Christopher (2000), *Twentieth-Century Irish Drama: Mirror up to Nation*, Syracuse, NY: Syracuse University Press.

Négrier, Emmanuel (2015), 'Festivalisation: Patterns and Limits', in Christopher Newbold, Christopher Maughan, Jennie Jordan, and Bianchini Franco (eds.), *Focus on Festivals: Contemporary European Case Studies and Perspectives*, Oxford: Goodfellow, pp. 18–27.

O'Brien, Eoin (1986), *The Beckett Country: Samuel Beckett's Ireland*, London: Faber and Faber.

O'Connell, Brenda and Nicholas Johnson (2014), 'Three Dialogues on Enniskillen', *The Beckett Circle*, Spring. www.researchgate.net/publication/307937544_Nicholas_Johnson_and_Brenda_O%27Connell_%27Three_dialogues_on_Enniskillen%27.

O'Reilly, Thomas (2012), note in the Happy Days Enniskillen International Beckett Festival programme, held by the author.

O'Toole, Fintan (2013), 'The Gatekeeper', *The Irish Times*, 30 November, p. 67.

Phelan, Peggy (1993), *Unmarked: The Politics of Performance*, London: Routledge.

Pilkington, Lionel (2001), *Theatre and State in Twentieth-Century Ireland: Cultivating the People*, London: Routledge.

Pine, B. Joseph and James Gilmore (2011), *The Experience Economy*, Boston, MA: Harvard Business Review.

Quinn, Bernadette (2010), 'Arts Festivals, Urban Tourism and Cultural Policy', *Journal of Policy Research in Tourism, Leisure and Events*, 2:3, pp. 264–79.

Rancière, Jacques (2004), *The Politics of Aesthetics: The Distribution of the Sensible*, trans. Gabriel Rockhill, London: Continuum.

Rancière, Jacques (2011), *The Emancipated Spectator*, London: Verso.

Rebellato, Dan (1999), *1956 and All That: The Making of Modern British Drama*, London: Routledge.

Richards, Greg and Palmer, Robert (2010), *Eventful Cities: Cultural Management and Urban Revitalization*, London: Elsevier.

Robinson, Lennox (1951), *Ireland's Abbey Theatre – A History 1899–1951*, London: Sidgwick and Jackson.

Samuels, Ellen (2017), 'Six Ways of Looking at Crip Time', *Disability Studies Quarterly*, 37:3. https://dsq-sds.org/article/view/5824/4684.

Scaife, Sarah Jane (2016), 'Practice in Focus: Beckett in the City', in Trish McTighe and David Tucker (eds.), *Staging Beckett in Ireland and Northern Ireland*, London: Methuen Bloomsbury, pp. 153–68.

Scott, Susie (2007), *Shyness and Society: The Illusion of Competence*, Basingstoke: Palgrave Macmillan.

Sharkey, Rodney (2021), 'Beckett's Present Moments', *Journal of Beckett Studies*, 30:1, pp. 8–25.

Siggins, Lorna (1986), 'Paris Marks Beckett's Birthday', *The Irish Times*, 1 April p. 10.

Simpson, Hannah (2018), 'Samuel Beckett and Nobel Catastrophe', *Samuel Beckett Today/Aujourd'hui*, 30, pp. 337–52.

Singleton, Brian (2004), 'The Revival Revised', in Shaun Richards (ed.), *The Cambridge Companion to Twentieth-Century Irish Drama*, Cambridge: Cambridge University Press, pp. 259–70.

Singleton, Brian (2016), 'Beckett and the Non-Place in Irish Performance', in Trish McTighe and David Tucker (eds.), *Staging Beckett in Ireland and Northern Ireland*, London: Methuen Bloomsbury, pp. 169–84.

Sisson, Elaine (2011), 'Experimentalism and the Irish Stage: Theatre and German Expressionism in the 1920s', in Linda King and Elaine Sisson (eds.), *Ireland, Design and Visual Culture: Negotiating Modernity, 1922–1992*, Cork: Cork University Press, pp. 39–58.

Smyth, Gerry (2001), *Space and Irish Cultural Imagination*, Basingstoke: Palgrave.

Snow, Georgia (2019), 'Edinburgh Fringe Ticket Sales Reach 3 Million for First Time', *Stage.com*, 27 August. www.thestage.co.uk/news/edinburgh-fringe-ticket-sales-reach-3-million-for-first-time.

Stallybrass, Peter and Allon White (1986), *The Politics and Poetics of Transgression*, Ithaca, NY: Cornell University Press.

Swift, Carolyn (1985), *Stage By Stage*, Dublin: Poolbeg.

Turk, Edward B. (2011), *French Theatre Today: The View from New York, Paris, and Avignon*, Des Moines: University of Iowa Press.

Turner, Victor (1987), 'Carnival, Ritual, and Play in Rio de Janeiro', in Alessandro Falassi (ed.), *Time Out of Time: Essays on the Festival*, Albuquerque: University of New Mexico Press, pp. 74–90.

Washburn, Martin (1996), 'Alive and Well', *Village Voice*, 20 August, p. 77.

Waterman, Stanley (1998), 'Carnivals for Élites? The Cultural Politics of Arts Festivals', *Progress in Human Geography*, 22:1, pp. 54–74.

Wehle, Phillipa (1984), 'A History of the Avignon Festival', *The Drama Review: TDR*, 28:1, pp. 52–61.

Whelan, Gerard (2002), *Spiked: Church-State Intrigue and 'The Rose Tattoo'*, Dublin: New Island.

Wilkie, Fiona (2002), 'Mapping the Terrain: A Survey of Site-Specific Performance in Britain', *New Theatre Quarterly*, 18:2, pp. 140–60.

Wilmer, Stephen E., ed. (1992), *Beckett in Dublin*, Dublin: Lilliput Press.

Wilmer, Stephen E. (2002), *Theatre, Society and the Nation: Staging American Identities*, Cambridge: Cambridge University Press.

Wilson Nightingale, Andrea (2004), *Spectacles of Truth in Classical Greek Philosophy: Theoria in its Cultural Context*, Cambridge: Cambridge University Press.

Wolf, Matt (1991), 'Just How Irish is Samuel Beckett?', *American Theatre*, review held at the Gate Theatre Dublin archives, PF77 c.

Woodworth, Paddy (1991), 'Playing Sam Again', *The Irish Times*, 28 September.

Zaiontz, Keren (2018), *Theatre and Festivals*, Basingstoke: Palgrave Macmillan.

Zaiontz, Keren (2020), 'From Post-War to "Second Wave": International Performing Arts Festivals', in Ric Knowles (ed.), *The Cambridge Companion to International Theatre Festivals*, Cambridge: Cambridge University Press, pp. 15–35.

Zuelow, Eric G. (2005), 'The Tourism Nexus: National Identity and the Meanings of Tourism since the Irish Civil War', in Mark McCarthy (ed.), *Ireland's Heritages: Critical Perspectives on Memory and Identity*, Aldershot: Ashgate, pp. 189–204.

Zukin, Sharon (1995), *The Culture of Cities*, Oxford: Blackwell.

Cambridge Elements ≡

Beckett Studies

Dirk Van Hulle

University of Oxford

Dirk Van Hulle is Professor of Bibliography and Modern Book History at the University of Oxford and director of the Centre for Manuscript Genetics at the University of Antwerp.

Mark Nixon

University of Reading

Mark Nixon is Associate Professor in Modern Literature at the University of Reading and the Co-Director of the Beckett International Foundation.

About the Series

This series presents cutting-edge research by distinguished and emerging scholars, providing space for the most relevant debates informing Beckett studies as well as neglected aspects of his work. In times of technological development, religious radicalism, unprecedented migration, gender fluidity, environmental and social crisis, Beckett's works find increased resonance. Cambridge Elements in Beckett Studies is a key resource for readers interested in the current state of the field.

Cambridge Elements ≡

Beckett Studies

Elements in the Series

Experimental Beckett: Contemporary Performance Practices
Nicholas E. Johnson and Jonathan Heron

Postcognitivist Beckett
Olga Beloborodova

Samuel Beckett's Geological Imagination
Mark Byron

Beckett and Sade
Jean-Michel Rabaté

*Beckett's Intermedial Ecosystems: Closed Space Environments across the Stage,
Prose and Media Works*
Anna McMullan

Samuel Beckett and Cultural Nationalism
Shane Weller

Absorption and Theatricality: On Ghost Trio
Conor Carville

Carnivals of Ruin: Beckett, Ireland, and the Festival Form
Trish McTighe

A full series listing is available at: www.cambridge.org/eibs

Lightning Source UK Ltd.
Milton Keynes UK
UKHW022206250123
415980UK00022B/197